The Teachings and Signs of Jesus in the Fourth Gospel

Craig Brian Manning

ISBN: 9781973158066

STUDIES PUBLISHED BY THIS AUTHOR

– *Jesus the Messiah and His Times*
Volume 1 – The Messiah and the Kingdom of Heaven
(E-Book and Paperback)

– *The Kingdom Parables of Jesus*
Volume 2 – The Messiah and the Kingdom of Heaven
(E-Book and Paperback)

– *The Return Parables and the Stories of Jesus*
Volume 3 – The Messiah and the Kingdom of Heaven
(E-Book and Paperback)

– *An Introduction to the Fourth Gospel*
Volume 1 – The Sevens of John
(E-Book and Paperback)

– *The Witnesses and Titles of Jesus in the Fourth Gospel*
Volume 2 – The Sevens of John
(E-Book and Paperback)

– *The Teachings and Signs of Jesus in the Fourth Gospel*
Volume 3 – The Sevens of John
(E-Book and Paperback)

– *The Revelations and DBR of Jesus in the Fourth Gospel*
Volume 4 – The Sevens of John
(E-Book and Paperback)

– *Great Figures of the Old Testament*
Volume 1 – Abraham, Joseph, and Moses
(E-Book and Paperback)

– *Great Figures of the Old Testament*
Volume 2 – In Process

– *A Concise History of the Chosen People*
(E-Book and Paperback)

– *Election or the Freedom to Choose*
(E-Book)

ABOUT THE AUTHOR

Craig Brian Manning is a life-long writer/editor. After receiving a Bachelor of Arts degree from Baylor University in Waco, Texas with a double major in Journalism and Religion, he began his career as a reporter/editor.

After working at several newspapers in north central Texas, he transitioned into technical writing which became his career. Mr. Manning has taught numerous adult Sunday school classes. He is an avid reader with an extensive library in Biblical studies and Christian doctrine.

Mr. Manning and his wife, Karen, are nearing their thirtieth wedding anniversary and have four adult children. The family attends a rural non-denominational church.

TABLE OF CONTENTS

CHAPTER ONE

INTRODUCTION

When Jesus began teaching about the kingdom of heaven; He introduced radically new ideas to the first-century Jewish world about the nature of God and how to relate to Him. He taught in a variety of settings ranging from one-on-one, as with Nicodemus and the woman at the well, to small groups such as the disciples or members of a synagogue He would often attend, to large groups of people numbering in the thousands. A gifted teacher, He was able to communicate with all sorts of people from many backgrounds—from the common to the artisan and from the barely literate to the learned.

Because He taught some two thousand years ago, many of the props or settings used to illustrate points or explain concepts are unfamiliar to us, although we may possess a basic understanding of them. For this reason, this study explores the world at the time of Jesus to help convey His message. These excerpts from the Fourth Gospel illustrate the depth and breadth of His teachings, which are as relevant today as when spoken two thousand years ago. One of the primary purposes of John is to present Jesus as the Messiah. Written about the same time as the Synoptic Gospels, this Gospel unlike the others, but presents Jesus as the Messiah by selecting various aspects of His earthly ministry. This study explores the seven signs, each of which reveals a facet of Jesus the Messiah.

"Much as one who holds a Ph.D. is expected to legitimate that status with learned discussions, so the Messiah is expected to show His identity by performing wonderful deeds." [1] The "signs" were proofs of His claims. This study, *The Teachings and Signs of Jesus in the Fourth Gospel*, is the third of four in the set titled *The Sevens of John*. The complete set includes:

- *An Introduction to the Fourth Gospel*
- *The Witnesses and Titles of Jesus in the Fourth Gospel*
- *The Teachings and Signs of Jesus in the Fourth Gospel*
- *The Revelations and DBR of Jesus in the Fourth Gospel*

CHAPTER TWO

THE FIRST TEACHING
THE NEW BIRTH

JOHN 3:1-36

The first teaching of Jesus in the Fourth Gospel occurred soon after He cleared the Temple of merchants and money changers. At this point in His earthly ministry, He was popular with the crowds and attracted attention from the religious authorities. Nicodemus, a member of the ruling council, came to Jesus to learn more of Him. What he discovered would change him to the point that he would later step forward to provide assistance at the death of Jesus the Messiah.

The identity of Nicodemus is unclear as there were several with the same name in the same general period.

Witherington suggests it is possible this man, besides being a leading member of the Sanhedrin, "was part of an illustrious family, for later a certain Gorion, son of a Nicodemus, negotiated with the Romans for the conclusion of the Jewish war." [2] That the meeting between Nicodemus and Jesus occurred at night should not be seen as subversive or furtive. Jesus was popular and most likely busy during the day with His ministry and dealing with the crowds.

Nicodemus came at night for the simple reason that this would provide the two men the best opportunity for a quiet conversation. However, the Fourth Gospel often associates light and day with Jesus and darkness with spiritual blindness and opposition to Jesus. John may have been inferring that, while Nicodemus came to Jesus at night for their mutual convenience, it also indicated his spiritual condition.

As a Pharisee, Nicodemus was not visiting Jesus to express outrage or concern about His clearing of the temple. It was likely he approved of the idea of clearing the merchants and moneychangers, especially since they were likely the Sadducees who were an opposing religious sect. Nicodemus opened the dialog in typical Jewish fashion with a compliment. In this instance, he said to Jesus, "You have come from God," which is a remarkable statement coming so early in the ministry of Jesus. The plural "you" is probably a reference to those members of the Sanhedrin who recognized Jesus as more than just a gifted teacher.

Some suggest Nicodemus brought several of his disciples along to meet Jesus, but most scholars dismiss this because the conversation in the Fourth Gospel was between two individuals. In verse eleven, Jesus also used the plural "we," but it is unclear whether He was referring to the disciples or the Father and Holy Spirit. Since this encounter happened early in the ministry of Jesus, it would have been unlikely His disciples would have seen enough for Jesus to include them in a plural reference; Jesus was likely referring to Himself, the Father, and the Holy Spirit.

Nicodemus, likely an older man since he was a member of the Sanhedrin and the teacher of Israel, displayed professional respect for Jesus by calling Him "Rabbi." He knew of and possibly believed in the miracles of Jesus and how they signified that Jesus was more than just a teacher. Lenski observes that Nicodemus correctly connected the signs of Jesus as validation from God. One of the tests of a true prophet at the time of Jesus was the performing of signs or miracles, in this way showing that God was with the individual. Even though the Fourth Gospel records only one miracle occurring in Jerusalem, the Apostle John notes that Jesus had performed other signs not included in his Gospel, and it is to those that Nicodemus referred.

Some see Nicodemus as a type representing the educated, religious, and devout Jew. The original language suggests his education and knowledge was the equivalent of a doctorate today. "It is remarkable that this highly respected Jewish teacher would honor the youngish (about thirty years old) Jesus as a fellow rabbi, especially since Jesus was known to lack formal rabbinic training." [3] As Phillips notes, this ruler of the Jews was the best the society and culture of Jerusalem could produce, and he was likely a good and moral man; Jesus quickly revealed, however, just how far Nicodemus was from the kingdom of heaven.

In response to the words of His visitor, Jesus opened with the double amen, which we translate, "truly, truly," indicating the importance of His words. Incidentally, His use of the double amen made Him distinctive among rabbis and teachers at the time; it was, in a sense, His signature statement. The polite words of Nicodemus to Jesus, while not containing a specific question, did contain within them an implied query about the identity of Jesus. As Carson notes, Nicodemus was seeking to define the parameters by which to evaluate Jesus and determine the legitimacy of His ministry.

Jesus rejected the premise of Nicodemus and insisted a person had to born again, or he or she could not be of the kingdom of heaven. "Thus, right at the beginning it is stated uncompromisingly that man, as he is, is excluded from salvation, from the sphere of God; for man, as he is, there is no possibility of it." [4] The concept of the kingdom of heaven was familiar to Nicodemus, although his understanding was different from that to which Jesus was referring. While the expression "kingdom of God" or "kingdom of heaven," as seen in Exodus 15:18, Psalm 93:1-2, and Psalm 103:19, it was taken to mean that God was the king or He reigns. Another view of the kingdom held by the Jews was that it would exist at the end of the age, with a descendant of David, a servant of God, as its king and Jerusalem as the capital. This perspective can be seen in Isaiah 9:7, Ezekiel 34:23-24, and Zachariah 9:9-10.

When Jesus began speaking to Nicodemus, He introduced the concept of being "born again." A more accurate translation for "born" may be "begotten," which, excluding the implication of human sexuality, means the same thing. Nicodemus would have been familiar with the meaning and context of the word. A typical translation of John 3:16 contain the word "begotten," and the same meaning is applicable in this instance. Scholars note that the phrase can also mean "born from above." Ridderbos argues the better interpretation be "born from above" and should be understood in the same way that Jesus came from above (3:13 and 3:31); this interpretation is likely correct given the context of the conversation between the two men.

The expression, "to be born again," should not have been unfamiliar to the renowned Jewish teacher. There are several instances of this term in Judaism; for example, "a Gentile on becoming a proselyte—though not, as has been suggested, an ordinary penitent—was likened to a child just born. It is also true that persons in certain circumstances—the bridegroom on his marriage, the Chief of the Academy on his promotion, the king on his enthronement—were likened to those newly born. The expression, therefore, was not only common, but, so to speak, fluid; only, both it and what it implied must be rightly understood." [5]

Seemingly not understanding what Jesus was saying or purposefully misunderstanding in an attempt to gain additional insight, Nicodemus asked how a man could be born again by his mother, referring to a physical act. Interestingly, he did not question *why* must one be born again, but *how,* and this may be significant for it suggests he wanted to learn more, rather than asking *why*, which is a more interrogative approach. Borchert suggests the reaction by Nicodemus is understandable since the manner in which Jesus expressed entering the kingdom of heaven was something His visitor did not expect.

This topic of discussion and the fact that Nicodemus did not know Jesus likely contribute to the confusion. It is noteworthy that Nicodemus even though shaken by the words of Jesus, maintained his poise and was not upset with this young rabbi who had swept aside his humble opening words along with the theological underpinnings upon which his faith rested. Despite all this, he continued his conversation with Jesus to learn more about what Jesus meant.

Some scholars take a Hellenistic approach to explaining the confusion of Nicodemus, supposing Jesus utilized a type of vertical dualism, implying in the statement "from above" the earth of down below. This view is incorrect because it over-emphasizes Greek influence and minimizes the Judaic perspective. By the time of Jesus, Judaism had a four-tier hermeneutical system to study the Old Testament and to counter the intellectual appeal of Greek thought. The four tiers contained the p'shat or simple, a straightforward factual statement; the remez, a word or phrase that hints back to another passage in Scripture; the d'rash, a deeper, spiritual interpretation with typological, homiletical, or allegorical application of the words; and the sod, a numerical analysis of Scripture in Hebrew to reveal meanings.

As a Pharisee, the teacher of Israel, and a member of the Sanhedrin, Nicodemus would have known of the four-level method to exegete Scripture. H chose to purposefully take the words Jesus spoke of being born again at the p'shat, or simple, level rather than the d'rash, or spiritual, meaning. The two men were exchanging ideas on different levels. We can see the response of Nicodemus as a rebuke or insult by receiving the words of Jesus at the p'shat level and responding in kind. It is likely that Nicodemus responded as he did to solicit a more in-depth explanation. Regardless of the reason behind the response of Nicodemus, Jesus explained what He meant; not an auspicious beginning to a theological conversation.

Jesus again began with the double amen, or "truly, truly," which emphasized His words and the need for the listener to listen. It is noteworthy that in this verse and verse three are the only times the phrase "kingdom of God" is found in the Fourth Gospel ("kingdom of heaven" never appears). Water was understood at the time of Jesus to refer to cleansing or purification. John the Baptist practiced baptism by water and the disciples of Jesus also baptized new believers. The practice of baptism was known at the time of Jesus but with different connotations than those of Jesus and His disciples. Spirit was understood to mean power, so neither baptism nor Spirit was a new concept to Nicodemus. It was the combination to gain entrance to the kingdom of heaven that was new and different to Nicodemus.

Nicodemus revealed his confusion in verses five and six when he questioned Jesus about physical rebirth. Jesus' technique of responding with a different level of meaning to the words of another person served to lead the conversation and to encourage the other person to reevaluate both Jesus and His words. With the hermeneutic system of the day, it was not difficult to jump back and forth between the p'shat, remez, and d'rash, conversing about the same topic but from different perspectives.

Jesus obliged Nicodemus and repeated what He had said with slightly different words. Jesus was trying to move Nicodemus away from the p'shat or simple level to the d'rash level of spiritual understanding and insight. He opened in the same manner as before and explained that, when He taught a person had to be born again by water and by the Spirit, He did not speak of the physical realm but the spiritual. Jesus explained the two levels of existence: the physical where flesh is born of flesh and the spiritual where the spirit is born of the Spirit. Because of the first Adam, fallen man could not produce anything but fallen offspring. That is why a new birth from the Spirit is necessary to obtain spiritual life.

Jesus also emphasized the exclusivity of the kingdom of heaven by saying a person could not "enter" the kingdom of heaven, whereas before He had said one could not "see" the kingdom. He repeated the requirement that a person must be born again and explained the mysteriousness of the Spirit and how no one knows of the Spirit, its activity, or where it goes. "The central idea is that the wind is also a mystery as to its origin and goal, but it still remains a reality, perceptible by means of its sound, recognizable through its effects." [6] Humans cannot predict the movement of the Holy Spirit. In the same way, people cannot understand those born of the Spirit. Nicodemus expressed his incredulity at the words of Jesus and asked how these things could be. Here was the "teacher of Israel" at a loss to understand what Jesus was trying to communicate. Jesus was taking what Nicodemus knew from the Old Testament and applying new meaning and insight, but Nicodemus was unable to comprehend.

"Nothing Jesus can say will clarify the matter or enlighten Nicodemus because he is flesh, who does not even know matters of flesh and earth." [7] The meaning of what Nicodemus said is unclear when he asked how these things could be. He could have been giving a figurative reply to what he perceived to be a figurative question or asking how a man of his age could so radically change his ways and lifestyle.

These verses also contain a reversal in that Nicodemus came to Jesus thinking he knew, but in the end, he did not, in fact, know. In just a few short verses, Jesus reduced this teacher of Israel to confusion and denial. Kostenberger opines that the second question reveals frustration on the part of Nicodemus. For him, admission to the kingdom of heaven focused on the actions of man—obedience to God's commandments and laws, submission to the will of God and deference to God—but now Jesus was telling him the only way to gain admittance to the kingdom was to be born again.

Jesus rebuked Nicodemus and asked if he could not understand when the topic was earthly things, how he could understand heavenly things. It is not clear what Jesus meant by this rebuke. There are three components in this conversation: the kingdom of heaven, the sonship of God, and eternal life. All of these are dependent upon perfect obedience to God, which is why something else is necessary. "It is just here that the idea of being reborn comes in. It is what links all three conceptions together." [8] To be reborn by the Spirit is the only way we can achieve entrance into the kingdom of heaven. The reason Jesus was able to speak of both earthly and heavenly things is that He, alone, was of heaven and of the world.

After Jesus had explained the "why" of being born again, He revealed the "how." After rebuking Nicodemus for his inability to believe earthly things, Jesus told him the One who descends from heaven, namely Himself, was the "how" to be saved. Only the One who came down from heaven could save. Jesus then explained how His death was the sacrifice for sin and cited Numbers 21:4-9, which tells of the Israelites constantly complaining in the Wilderness and being punished by God. As Barclay succinctly explains, it was not the bronze serpent that saved; it was merely a symbol to help the stricken Israelites turn their thoughts back to God.

By the power of God, they were healed. In the same way, Jesus explained He would be lifted up, and those who looked to Him would be saved, but in a spiritual nature. The phrase "lifted up" is found four times in this Gospel, and each time it means a physical lifting of a body on a cross. Even the prophet Isaiah spoke the word picture of being lifted up and ascribed a spiritual connotation as the suffering servant. Nicodemus, of all people, should have understood what Jesus said, even though He spoke from the d'rash perspective. We cannot say for certain from the narrative whether Nicodemus became a believer. The evidence seems to support the idea that he came to a saving faith, given that he sought fair and equitable treatment of Jesus and assisted with the burial of Jesus.

Most scholars believe John appends the rest of the third chapter to summarize the conversation and to reinforce basic concepts of salvation through Jesus. Verse sixteen is, of course, one that many have memorized as children in church or vacation bible school, and it is often spoken in witness and outreach.

CHAPTER THREE

THE FIRST SIGN
TURNING WATER INTO WINE

JOHN 2:1-11

Jesus performed the first sign soon after He started His ministry, although we are unable to precisely determine the time. This sign revealed the authority of Jesus over quality. In addition to revealing an aspect of His messianic claims, this passage reveals much of His compassion and provides insight to the social fabric of the time. The passage opens with the phrase "And on the third day," which places the wedding at Cana within a timeline.

That John opened the narrative in this manner signifies some importance of the events before the wedding, "Although it is tempting to imagine the evangelist mapping out a cosmic week as in Genesis 1, the data does not support this. It seems more profitable to interpret 'the third day' as a transition from times of testimony and recruitment to times of 'signs,' that is, a different aspect of Jesus' career." [9]

The passage simply chronicles events from the beginning days of His ministry and His gathering disciples to the first sign of turning water into wine. As with the other signs, some question whether the event is factual. Bultmann, for example, writes "there can be no doubt that the story has been taken over from heathen legend and ascribed to Jesus. In fact, the motif of the story, the changing of the water into wine, is a typical motif of the Dionysus legend." [10] There are others who seek to cast aspersions on this and the other signs, but few with the intensity of Bultmann.

Going back to the first day of the timeline (John 1:19), a delegation of religious leaders from Jerusalem came to John the Baptist to question his messianic proclamations. On the second day, Jesus came to John the Baptist for baptism following the forty days of temptation, and John declared Jesus to be the Lamb of God. The next day Andrew and probably John met Jesus and became His disciples. That they stayed with Jesus for the day suggests it was a Sabbath with restrictions on how far a person could travel. On the fourth day, Andrew introduced his brother, Simon, to Jesus. The next day Jesus met Nathanael.

Nothing significant happened on the sixth day, but this was likely the time necessary for Jesus and His new disciples to walk to Cana for the wedding. The first sign occurred on the seventh day. The reference to Cana in Galilee also indicates the village was relatively unknown. Of the locations discovered by archeologists, the most likely location of this community is Khirbet Cana, located on the Plains of Asochis about nine miles north of Nazareth. Josephus, in his writings, supports this site of the community.

The invitation of Jesus to the wedding indicates it was a family occasion. We can assume that at least one of the parties in the wedding was a family friend or relative of Mary and Jesus since both were invited. John does not mention Joseph, Mary's husband, which suggests Joseph may already have been dead. Assuming Joseph was in his late teens or early twenties when he and Mary were married, and that Jesus was now thirty years old, Joseph would have been around fifty, the life expectancy of the time. If Mary were younger by several years than her husband, typical for the time, she would have been in her mid to late forties.

Some have asked how Jesus came to be invited to the wedding. One possibility is that Jesus, on the way to Cana, stopped at Nazareth, where He received notification of the coming wedding. Another option is that Nathanael, who was from Cana, invited Jesus and the disciples. Lenski notes the invitation to Jesus included the disciples, implying that the inviting person knew of His ministry and followers. At this time, Jesus had five disciples—Andrew, Simon, Philip, Nathanael, and John.

Weddings were a time of celebration and festivities. If the bride were a virgin, the wedding took place on Wednesday; if the bride were a widow, on Thursday. The bridegroom and his party would make a procession to the home of the bride. Typically, this was done at night so torches would have been necessary to light the way, which, of course, attracted attention and added to the excitement. The parable of the Ten Virgins explains the role of the bridegroom and his party as well as the preparations made by the bride and her attendants.

After the ceremony, they threw a party lasting as long as a week depending on the wealth and extravagance of the groom and his family. "Each day new guests would appear. Much food and wine were consumed, involving considerable financial strain upon the bridegroom, whose responsibility it was to provide for his guests." [11] The Greeks placed so much emphasis on the marriage feast that this event was sufficient to prove the legality of marriage.

At some point during the festivities, Mary learned or someone told her the supply of wine was exhausted. To run out of wine was a serious problem for the groom because he was expected to prepare sufficient food and drink for a considerable quantity to remain at the conclusion of the festivities. If the guests discovered there was no more wine, it would have been more than social embarrassment. There was a strong cultural emphasis on the concept of honor and shame, which influenced to some degree every component of a person's life, the private as well as the public.

In addition to the personal shame of running out of wine, there was the potential for litigation against the bridegroom and his family for failing to provide for the guests. While in today's world to run out of drink is more of an inconvenience, at the time of Jesus, the solution and ramifications were far more significant. Mary apparently had some role in the festivities because she took the initiative. A few scholars claim the unexpected presence of Jesus and His party was the reason the festivities consumed all of the wine, but the fact that Jesus and His followers were invited to the festivities negates this idea. These scholars have taken Mary coming to Jesus upon learning of the problem as support for the idea that Jesus and His disciples were the cause of the problem. "There is no evidence to support the speculation that the reason the wine ran out was because Jesus arrived at the last moment with a crowd of followers who had not been anticipated." [12]

Speculation abounds as to the reason Mary came to Jesus with this problem. Suggestions range from selfish motivation to her seeking to encourage Jesus to proclaim His identity to the world. Likely the actual reason Mary turns to her son was that He had proven to be competent in solving problems during the years

He lived under her authority before departing to begin His ministry. However, the relationship between the two had irrevocably changed since her Son had left home several months before the wedding. When Jesus addressed Mary with the salutation of "woman," we should not take this greeting as rude or abrupt. This type of salutation was the same manner by which Odysseus addressed Penelope, his wife. It was also how Augustus, Emperor of Rome, addressed Cleopatra, the queen of Egypt. Rather than being discourteous or rude, the salutation was, in fact, an expression of respect.

It was a common form of speech, and Jesus used the same expression when He provided for her care by the Apostle John at the crucifixion. "The original idiom of Jesus' reply involves no disrespect but stresses His acquiescence to God's sovereign timing." [13] Unknown to her, Jesus was forging a new relationship, and she had to learn she could no longer presume her wishes would be predominating in the decisions of Jesus. "It is here quite unlikely that Jesus was expressing hostility to his mother, but the statement does seem to imply that he wanted to set straight the parameters of his public relationship with her."

His reply to Mary is puzzling because He rebuffed her request for assistance and commented that His hour had not yet come. His response was "marking a certain contrast, which, however, can take on various nuances according to the contest—and the tone of voice." [14] The essential point of His statement was that He "does not permit Himself to be prompted to act by any human agent, even when that agent is His own mother; He is driven by the will of the Father alone." [15] It is worth noting the passage mentions not the mother of Jesus. "John's omission of the name of Mary may have been part of his divine inspiration. Various Gnostic and cultic errors were already taking deep root in the church. The day would come when the Roman Catholic Church would proclaim Mary as having been immaculately conceived, free from original sin. In the fertile imagination of men and by false church dogma she would be exalted bodily to heaven, and the devout would be asked to believe in her corporeal presence there." [16]

The act of providing divine intervention was a critical crossroad for Jesus. "If He performed this miracle, and manifested forth His glory, He would become the gazing stock of every eye, and the common talk of every tongue. He would be followed about from place to place, thronged and jostled by vulgar crowds. This action would provoke the jealously of religious leaders, and He would be spied upon and regarded as a public menace. Later, this would eventuate in His being seized as a notorious criminal, falsely accused, and sentenced to be crucified." [17] Jesus made His decision and acted. At the wedding, there were six stone water pots for ceremonial washing. The water pots were of stone, which could not attract uncleanliness and was more impermeable than pottery or earthenware.

As Mark 7:3-4 explains, everyone understood the contents of the water pots were for purification rather than mere consumption. The amount of water in the six water pots was approximately 100 to 150 gallons, sufficient for a relatively large number of people to wash their hands in preparation for a meal. Jesus commanded the servants to fill the containers with water. The servants retrieved water from the nearby well and filled the water pots to the brim until, according to the narrative, it was not possible to add more. The original language indicates there was a well nearby.

Jesus commanded some water be drawn and taken to the headwaiter or master of ceremonies. The master sampled what was now wine and called the bridegroom to compliment him on the wine. He also commented while most served the best wine first and then, after the guests were inebriated and less able to discern the quality of the wine, served the poorer-quality refreshments. "The sign is only semi-public, for only the servants, Mary, and the disciples seem to know how this had taken place and who had done it." [18] Despite the relatively few who knew, the Gospel notes the disciples believed in Jesus. While the level of belief was likely not what Jesus sought, it was a beginning and a necessary step for the new disciples. As would be the case in most of His works, some who were present were not aware of the sign while those Jesus desired to be aware believed in Him. As Morris notes, His glory was revealed to some and hidden to others.

Wine was a standard component of daily life at the time of Jesus. Entire villages focused on the production of wine, and it was an important industry in Galilee. Wine did not contain the potency of wine today because the fermentation and wine-making process were cruder and thus, while wine did have some intoxicating effect, the impact was minimal. They did have "strong" wine as noted in Proverbs, but it was intended for the seriously injured or dying and was comparable to the wines of today that contain an alcohol content of anywhere from seven to twelve percent. Apart from this purpose, social custom frowned on the consumption of strong wine.

Despite the characteristics of wine at the time of Jesus, some have difficulty accepting the fact that Jesus provided wine and offer various alternatives. However, to claim the wine was some form of grape juice or a form of non-alcoholic beverage tests the limits of credulousness. In that part of the world, grapes ripened from June to September. Thus, the argument that the wine offered at weddings between October and May would not have been fermented wine does not have merit. While the alcohol content of the wine at the time of Jesus was considerably less potent than today, their wine contained a small percent of alcohol. The fact that this occurred "at a wedding and is designed to prevent serious social embarrassment marks Jesus out as far removed from the monastic asceticism of hermitic communities like Qumran." [19]

In the Old Testament, wine represents joy, whereas, at the first sign, the wine was running out. This was an accurate allegory of Judaism; it existed, but offered little or no comfort or hope, for it had become a mechanical, cold ritual far from the love and grace of God. The amount of wine Jesus provided the wedding ceremony was an indicator of the joy of the kingdom. We should understand the prominence of the water pots to represent Judaism. Since the Jews believed seven was the perfect number, six was short of perfection. In the same way, the six stone water pots "stand for the entire system of Jewish ceremonial observance—and by implication for religion upon that level, wherever it is found," [20] as opposed to what Jesus was inaugurating.

The filling of the water pots to the brim signified the fulfillment of the old religion and that it was not possible to add to it. The Jewish religion had completed its purpose, and it was time for the new. The arrival and ministry of Jesus would make the number of water pots seven, since Jesus was the living water, representing the fulfillment of the Jewish faith. "What was lacking at the wedding was wine, not water, the water of the law. The jars needed at the wedding were to meet the requirements of the law and were requisitioned to remedy what threatened to turn the wedding feast into a big disappointment—the lack of wine." [21] The wine is the new, and the water is the old. "Knowing the mystical nature of John, one cannot help but see the inferred lesson. The 'wine' or way or life, which Jesus provides, is better than that which was available under the Law or under the Jewish system of religion." [22]

The author does not tell when the transformation occurred, but instead rather understates that the water turned into wine. He does not explain the amount of water which became wine, whether someone took just the cup to the head waiter, all of the water in the water pots, or if the water became wine as someone poured it out for to the guests. Most commentators suggest all of the water in the six stone water pots became wine, which means Jesus gave a generous gift to the couple. We do not find other seemingly important details in the account of this miracle. The name of the bride and groom are unknown, as is the name of the steward. The passage reveals little about the event itself—the size of the wedding party, the number of guests, what role Mary had in the wedding—but enough is provided to convey the account of the sign.

We can also interpret the rare act of saving the best wine for last as a living parable of Jesus. The first wine at the wedding banquet represented Judaism as known before the time of Jesus. The new wine represented the new form of belief as taught by Jesus. The wedding feast introduced the world to the taste of new wine. The place and occurrence of this first sign show how different from John the Baptist Jesus was. Rather than fasting and living as a hermit, Jesus was around people and was able to interact with others from differing social backgrounds and status.

The sign to turn water into wine was necessary, as Brown notes, to help reveal Jesus as the one sent to bring salvation. "This miracle, so different from those that were to come, resembles them in the most important point, for it too suggests by its very nature the kind of faith it is designed to inspire: a faith of fulfillment and of transformation, of joy and celebration." [23] In this passage, "several details of the narrative remind the reader of Jesus' little 'parable' of new wine requiring new wineskins. The newness and joy of the kingdom's arrival are vividly depicted." [24]

While the couple and, indirectly, Mary, were the beneficiaries of this sign, the underlying purpose was to lead the new disciples to believe in Jesus. To think the disciples put their faith in Him because of a joke or prank is to cast aspersion on both these men and Jesus. John says twice, verses nine and eleven, the water turned into wine, so the idea the liquid remained water conflicts with the Gospel of John. The turning of water into wine symbolizes the transforming power of Jesus.

CHAPTER FOUR

THE SECOND TEACHING
THE WATER OF LIFE

JOHN 4:1-29

After the Passover and the meeting between Jesus and Nicodemus, Jesus, and His disciples, left Judea and returned to Galilee. While most devout Jews went out of their way to avoid traveling through Samaria, which was between Judea and Galilee, Jesus chose to pass through it. When they arrived at Jacob's well at the village of Sychar about noon, they stopped, and Jesus sent the disciples into the nearby town to obtain food. Jesus was resting alone when a Samaritan woman came to the well to draw water.

During this period of His earthly ministry, the Pharisees were beginning to oppose Him because of the number of people who were listening to His message. Correctly, they perceived Him to be a greater threat than John the Baptist. Due in part to this and His desire to minister in Galilee, Jesus and His disciples left for Galilee. The route to the north, as the passage notes, meant it was necessary for Him to travel through Samaria, a three-day journey, via the road known as the Ancient Way of the Patriarchs.

Typically, Jewish travelers bypassed the region and went east through the Transjordan, a predominately Gentile area, travelled across the Jordan River, and then turned back to the west to Galilee. The reason for this tortuous route between Judea and Galilee was the animosity between the Jews and Samaritans. The inhabitants of the region—Jews and Samaritans alike—maintained an unspoken separateness with the Jews to the North, who lived in Galilee, and to the south, who lived in Judea. Devout Jews wanted nothing to do with Samaritans, and the Samaritans held similar views toward the Jews. That the Gospel infers it was "necessary" or that He "had" to pass through Samaria (different translations use a similar expression), implies He was divinely led to take this route rather than taking the more circuitous route.

As the group walked northward, they arrived at Jacob's well, which was at a fork in the old Roman road just south of Sychar, now known as Askar. One fork went to Capernaum and the other to Nazareth. The well was about a half mile from Sychar and several hundred yards from Joseph's tomb. The ancient city of Shechem was also close by, at the entrance of the valley that separates Mount Gerizim and Mount Ebal. Since the well was about one hundred feet deep, access to water was impossible except by a bucket or container lowered from the top of the well. The person seeking water typically brought his or her own vessel. Buckets or animal-skin containers were not available to a stranger because of cultural and religious reasons. Why Jacob dug the well at this location is unknown, especially since there was a nearby spring always containing water. It could have been for convenience or possibly that Jacob sought to avoid trouble with his neighbors.

It was about the noon hour, and Jesus was weary and hungry. "If Jesus had been baptizing in the same area as John the Baptist and had left from there heading north-west to Sychar, He has covered a significant distance. As the crow flies, Sychar is about thirty miles from Aenon; but following the Roman roads, it is about forty miles. The journey would take a day and a half, so Jesus and His disciples would arrive in Sychar on the second day at about the sixth hour." [25] Being fatigued, He sent the disciples into the nearby town to purchase food. The inclusion of Jesus' physical needs by the Apostle John is not accidental. "The strategic Christian doctrine of the incarnation is not merely a theological assertion about the deity of Jesus; it is equally an assertion about his humanity." [26] As He was human, Jesus knew all the emotions and feelings we experience: physical weariness, hunger, and thirst.

"This simple question began one of the classic soul-winning efforts of all times. In Jerusalem, Jesus had dealt with Nicodemus, an honored man in Jewish society. Now He is dealing with a woman of shame in Samaritan society." [27] The encounter between Jesus and the Samaritan woman continues several themes of the previous chapter, including water and the fulfillment of Old Testament messianic prophecies. Nicodemus typified the Orthodox Jew; the woman at the well typified the opposite extreme. For the Orthodox Jew, the individual at the well had three insurmountable strikes: she was Samaritan, female, and guilty of sexual sins, which placed her at the opposite end of the social spectrum from Nicodemus. There are other notable contrasts between Nicodemus and the Samaritan woman; one met Jesus at night, the other at noon; one was cautious, the other bold; and one asking questions, the other debating. In the course of two passages, John masterfully reveals Jesus being for all people regardless of social or financial status, education, religion, sex, or personal integrity.

Jesus had sent the disciples into Sychar, the nearby town, to acquire food, leaving Him alone at the well. On the top of the well was a parapet of stone or wood upon which the weary would rest. Jews did have some dealings with Samaritans, but there were numerous prohibitions of behaviors implemented by the Pharisees to avoid ceremonial uncleanliness. These were such things as not accepting certain kinds of food or sharing a common vessel to drink water. That Jesus sent His disciples to the Samaritan town for food indicates they were not as strict as some about associating with Samaritans. At the time of Jesus, dry food was accepted as more likely to be contaminated by Samaritans than other types of food, such as soups or other prepared foods. Later rabbinical regulations, even more strict than during the time of Jesus, banned even the consumption of dry food.

It is not certain why the woman chose to get water from Jacob's well when there was water readily available from other sources in the immediate area closer to her home. It may have been because of the depth of the well, because the water tasted better, or because she had a degree of reverence for the well because of the great patriarch associated with it. The reference to the sixth hour is typical in the Fourth Gospel and means noon. It is also noteworthy that the woman came alone to draw water during the hottest part of the day rather than at sunset, which was the more typical time for this task. "Women were more likely to come in groups to fetch water, and either earlier or later in the day when the heat of the sun was not so fierce." [28] This particular woman probably came to the well at this time because the other women shunned her. "Despite some Jewish polemic to the contrary, the Samaritans were intensely religious, and like other ancient Near Eastern and

Mediterranean peoples, they took seriously a woman's sexual immorality." [29]

When the Samaritan woman approached the well, Jesus initiated the conversation and requested a drink of water. According to the Pharisees, this was improper as He did not have a vessel to draw or drink the water, and the Samaritan would have to provide something from which He could drink, which would make Him ceremonially unclean. That Jesus would even be in her presence, much less talk to her, broke serious social and religious barriers. Rabbinical regulations forbade a rabbi from speaking to a woman—even his wife—in public. Because this woman was notorious, "no decent man, let alone a rabbi, would have been seen in her company, or even exchanging a word with her—and yet Jesus spoke to her." [30]

Likely shocked, the woman immediately referred to the long-standing Samaritan and Jewish conflict and asked why He, a Jew, would think to ask her, a Samarian woman, for water. Despite the seeming impossibility of such a conversation, the Apostle John records that she spoke to Jesus six times and once to the inhabitants of her village while Jesus spoke seven times to her—seven representing perfect in Scripture. As Jesus did with Nicodemus, He took the starting point, in this case, water, and replied on a deeper—the d'rash level. She responded to His request for water with the basic type of communication, the p'shat, which would be expected given the nature of the request.

Jesus used the response of the woman to explain to her that, if she knew who was speaking to her, she would instead have asked for the gift of living water. The Apostle John emphasizes the gift of the living water that it is free. "Living water" meant water in a stream or river in contrast to water in a well or cistern that did not flow. In the context of the conversation, there is a spiritual or religious connotation. "In Judaism, 'spring water' (living water) is primarily a figure for Yahweh Himself and the salvation that proceeds from Him." [31]

While Jesus did not refer to a specific Old Testament passage, we can find the concept or theme He was conveying in passages such as Isaiah 58:11 and Zechariah 14:8. Jeremiah 2:13 and Jeremiah 17:13 also contain similar passages. In this way, Jesus directed the conversation to the d'rash level or the spiritual, which caused momentary confusion on the part of the woman, who responded as anyone would have to such a change in the focus of a conversation. "It was 'living water' that took away defilement and made acceptable worshippers out of unclean people." [32]

The woman responded to Jesus using "Sir," by which she could have been trying to establish distance from Jesus. The woman "shows no sign of understanding what Jesus is talking about and, like Nicodemus and the disciples later, clings to the literal meaning of Jesus' words." [33] She refused to participate in a spiritual conversation and remained focused, whether innocent or purposeful, on the physical water in the well from which she drew the water. Her perspective is evident when she asked Him how He proposed to draw the "living water" since the well was deep. A spring fed Jacob's well, and the term "living water" could also mean "running water," which is likely how the woman understood Jesus. Thinking this stranger could not be more important than the man who dug the well; she asked if He were greater than Jacob. If He could not produce this "living water," she could dismiss Him as a false prophet. The construction of her question suggests she expected the stranger would be proven false. However, she provided Jesus the perfect opportunity to present a message of salvation.

Despite the challenging and possibly boisterous attitude of the woman, Jesus continued in the same vein and explained the difference between the water from the well, which would only result in more thirst, and living water, which would become a spring leading to eternal life. At this point, Jesus began to speak more clearly of the differences between the two waters that were so confusing the Samaritan woman.

Again, the connection between drawing water and eternal life has hints or remez to Messianic prophetic passages like Isaiah 12:3, Isaiah 44:3, and Isaiah 49:10. The woman would probably not have recognized these verses because the Samaritans did not accept the Old Testament beyond the first five books written by Moses, the Pentateuch. Jesus also hinted to Jeremiah 31:23-24 and Joel 2:28-32 about the living water welling up to eternal life, which, again, the woman would probably not have discerned, but those familiar with the Jewish Old Testament would have noticed.

The Samaritan woman is an example of one trying to focus on the physical instead of the spiritual. The technique of Jesus of responding on a different level of hermeneutical meaning—usually the third level d'rash (spiritual) to the p'shat (simple)—seems to have been a tactic to lead and direct the other person to reevaluate both Jesus and his or her contribution to the conversation. As a note, Jesus would hint to verses in the Old Testament that contain relevant ideas or principles He was trying to convey.

That the Samaritan woman was naturally not very knowledgeable of the Jewish Old Testament while Jesus was intimately familiar with these passages explains the type of conversation between the two. The different level of conversation is evident in her statement, "Give me this water, so I will not be thirsty, nor come all the way here to draw." As Barclay notes, there are truths that one cannot be told, that the person must discover for him- or herself. With the hermeneutical system of the time, it was not difficult to switch between p'shat, remez, and d'rash all while discussing the same topic.

At this point, the conversation had evidently not yet produced the results Jesus sought, probably because the woman was not noticing or was ignoring, the subtle messianic references in His words. He then revealed divine knowledge about her life. Morris notes that up to this point in the conversation the woman was not serious but was humoring Him. However, when He asked her to call her husband and return, the conversation suddenly became serious and threatening because she realized the man with whom she was conversing knew more about her than He should.

In an attempt to conceal herself and also maintain distance in a social sense, she tersely responded to the request in as few words as possible. Her reply was truthful and deceitful. There is likely a close connection between her request for the "living water" and Jesus' request for her to go and bring back her husband. "Does this woman desire living water? Then there must be a thirst for this water. This thirst will not be truly awakened unless there be a sense of guilt, a consciousness of sin. The mention of her husband is the best means of reminding this woman of her immoral life." [34]

The woman, surely defensive at this point in the conversation, replied truthfully and said she had no husband. Jesus gave her faint praise for the technical truth of her words, and she probably thought her avoidance of the question had been successful. However, He then revealed that He knew she had had five husbands, and the man with whom she was living was not her husband. So, yes, the woman spoke the truth, but also a falsehood.

Some scholars suggest the number of husbands was a reference to the syncretistic cults of the Samaritans, but this has been found to be another illustration of extreme interpretation, regardless how it is interpreted or constructed. Other scholars argue that the five husbands are an allegorical reference to the Pentateuch or the five peoples who were brought in by the Assyrians after the Jews were exiled to Babylon, but neither of these stands the scrutiny of close examination as Brown notes in his commentary. Jesus adroitly turned her words against her and forced her to confront her sin so He could present the gift of salvation. Jesus was not seeking to condemn the woman, but He had to force her to face the reality of her many relationships so she would be open to God, the Father.

That Jesus knew about her many husbands and that the man with whom she was living was not her legal husband prompted her to realize the man with whom she was conversing was more than just a man. She admitted this when she called Jesus a prophet, which was a man sent by God to deliver His message. Note the progression in the woman's addresses to Jesus. She first referred to Him as a "Jew," then "Sir," and now "Prophet." In a sense, her reaction is similar to that of Nathanael when Jesus told him He had seen him while he was sitting under a fig tree (John 1:48). As she learned more about this man, the words with which she addressed Him reveal dawning revelation. The

Samaritans only believed in the first five books of the Old Testament, which taught there would be only one great prophet after Moses—the Taheb, the Samaritan term for Messiah. If her motives were honest, she was on the verge of an astonishing discovery.

In a change of topic that may have been a genuine question or a diversion, the woman asked Jesus whether worship was appropriate at Mount Gerizim or the Jerusalem Temple. This question seems to have been an attempt to trap Jesus and force an answer that would indicate the superiority of either the Jewish or Samaritan religious viewpoint. As a brief note of explanation, the Samaritans and Jews had a long history of animosity extending back to pre-exilic times.

One of the results of the exile was that those who went into exile took the opportunity to re-evaluate their religion and write numerous books that became part of their Old Testament. Those who were left behind kept only the Pentateuch and did not accept the legitimacy of the additional books. Also, the two groups disagreed on where God chose to build the Temple. The Samaritans understood Deuteronomy 12:5 to refer to Mount Gerizim while the returning exilic Jews thought Jerusalem the most appropriate location for the Temple. Jesus was seemingly in a no-win situation; any response could offend someone, but His response negated her challenge and gave Him the opportunity to answer her sincere question.

Jesus responded to the question with a three-part answer. The manner in which Jesus spoke to the Samaritan woman is interesting; as Haenchen notes, Jesus addressed her as "woman," which is the same expression He used toward His mother Mary both at the wedding at Cana and at the cross. His answer made irrelevant the issue of whether worship at Mount Gerizim or in Jerusalem was an issue; salvation came from the Jews, inferring it did not originate from the Samaritans; and the new worship of God was not confined to the Temple or sacred mountain but was possible anywhere. "The Gospel displays no hatred of the Jewish people though it regards them with a certain aloofness. The role of Israel in the history of salvation is not denied, but considered as a stage that has been left behind." [35]

This answer by Jesus was based on the Pentateuch, which the Samaritans believed. With regard to the proper place to worship God, Jesus meant the time was coming and had, in fact, arrived in which neither Mount Gerizim nor Jerusalem could claim to be the exclusive location for worship. This announcement was another indicator of Jesus inaugurating the spiritual kingdom of heaven.

Jesus answered the question and completely settled the argument. "The heart of the story appears in 4:23-24: the Father has been seeking true worshippers who will worship Him in spirit and truth, and that was why the Father sent Jesus to this woman. Outward markers, which John's religious contemporaries would contemplate, such as her gender, religious tradition and ethnicity, and past moral activity, prove irrelevant in revealing the sort of person God seeks to worship Him." [36] The woman had no reply to what Jesus says.

Due to His insight into her life, His answer about worship, and likely His demeanor toward her, she reached an improbable conclusion: could this man possibly be the promised Messiah? She expressed her understanding that she knew, much as Nicodemus knew, that the Messiah, who would declare all things, was coming. That the Samaritans only accepted the first five books of the Old Testament meant their understanding of the Messiah was limited, and her messianic expectations revealed this deficiency. Despite her limited understanding, she anticipated the coming of the Messiah. Perhaps not knowing the response she would receive, she posed an open-ended question about the Messiah in a way Jesus could answer as He saw appropriate.

Jesus responded calmly to her statement about the coming Messiah, saying simply, "I, who speak to you, am He." This occasion was the one time Jesus declared Himself the Messiah except during His trial. He could not have said such a thing to the Jews because "the title Messiah carried so much political and military baggage that His self-disclosure in such settings necessarily had to be more subdued and subtle." [37] This caution was because if He made the claim to the Jews, they would have misunderstood what He was trying to communicate or believed He was seeking to initiate a revolution against the Romans. In the rural areas as well as in Samaria, where the people were more down to earth, Jesus could use more direct words.

CHAPTER FIVE

THE SECOND SIGN
HEALING THE NOBLEMAN'S SON

JOHN 4:46-54

The second sign shows the authority of Jesus to heal and His authority over distance. Jesus spoke the healing words in Cana, and the child was healed in Capernaum. As with all the signs, this reveals another facet of the Messianic credentials of Jesus. This sign took place in the same village where He had turned water into wine. The return to Galilee after His trip to Jerusalem marked the beginning of His Galilean ministry, which lasted from December 27 to April 29 CE. The region of Galilee was under the control of Herod Antipas, one of the sons of Herod the Great.

According to the Fourth Gospel, after the wedding in Cana, Jesus and His disciples went to Capernaum to be with His mother, brothers, and sisters before traveling to Jerusalem for the Passover. It was at this Passover that Jesus, the first of two times, chased the merchants and moneychangers from the Temple (John 2:13-16). Following the Passover, Jesus and the disciples returned to Galilee passing through Samaria where He had His encounter with the Samaritan woman at the well. Upon leaving there, they returned to Cana where John, in a matter of fact manner, recalled that this was where Jesus had turned the water into wine. Morris notes that the first sign happened and was not an allegorical representation of the ministry of Jesus.

John noted when Jesus returned to Galilee, that the crowds welcomed Him. We can infer from this that those who live in the region know of Him. It is likely that many Galileans also went to Jerusalem for the Passover and were familiar with Jesus and His clearing of the Temple. It is probably correct to say "many Galilean pilgrims to the temple were annoyed at the way of the temple establishment or merchants acted; in any case, it reinforces the cultural divide between Judea and Galilee implied throughout this Gospel and the Gospel tradition." [38] The reputation of Jesus was surely already spreading, as more of a healer rather than the inaugurator of a new religion.

The revelation of the power of Jesus to cure the sick and to heal people was surely the reason the royal official came seeking help for his sick son. Jesus probably performed more healings or signs the Gospels record. How else would word so quickly spread among the villages and communities about this man Jesus who could heal the sick and infirm? The coming of crowds to Jesus confirmed what the Apostle John wrote at the conclusion of the Fourth Gospel: there were many other things Jesus did, which would fill volumes (John 21:25).

Most scholars believe the man who came seeking Jesus to heal his son was a mid-level official for Herod Antipas. "It would seem that this courtier was a Jew, for in 4:48 he is included in the multitude of Jews who were interested in Jesus chiefly as a miracle-worker." [39] The official from Capernaum had heard of Jesus and the stories about His powers. When his son's condition suddenly worsened, it prompted him to seek assistance from any source, including Jesus. Learning He was in the vicinity, the royal official traveled, probably by horse, to Cana for help for his son. The town of Capernaum is about twenty miles northwest of Cana and considerably lower than the surrounding region. The village is on the northwestern shore of the Sea of Galilee, which is about seven hundred feet below Cana. To explain the relationship between the two villages and the Sea of Galilee, Cana is about twenty miles west of the Sea of Galilee with Capernaum on the northern shore of the body of water.

The other Gospels tell of Jesus healing two people at a distance: the slave of the Centurion (Matthew 8:5-13,

Luke 7:2-10) and the daughter of the Syro-Phoenician (Matthew 15:21-28, Mark 7:24-30). The account of the healing of the royal official's son is somewhat similar to the account of the healing of the Centurion's slave. The rather harsh words Jesus spoke to those who would not believe without signs and wonders are similar to His reaction to the Syro-Phoenician woman. Because of these perceived similarities, some suggest the second sign is a variation of the healing of the Centurion's slave.

Schnackenburg evaluates the evidence as to whether the two events were originally the same incident. Citing the similarities between the two illnesses, the implied age of the sick persons, and the position of authority of the petitioners, he opines that this healing of the nobleman's son and the healing of the Centurion's slave are the same and that Luke and John took the basic event and wove different narratives. In reality, there are insufficient aspects of similarity between the two accounts outside of some verbal parallels and the fact Jesus healed at a distance. The Roman centurion was a Gentile; the royal official is thought to have been Jewish. The person in distress in one of the accounts was a slave; in the other account, the ill person was a young child. The centurion told Jesus He did not need to be present to heal his slave; the royal official insisted Jesus had to be in the presence of his son to heal. Yes, while there are general similarities, the verses that are remotely consistent fail to reach the level of persuasion that the account in Luke or the account in John was highly embellished and that the accounts were of the same healing.

When Jesus and His disciples returned to Cana, the site of the first sign, the man apparently learned He was there and left Capernaum to seek out Jesus. "News of Jesus' wonderful signs in Jerusalem had been spread throughout Galilee by pilgrims returning from the recent Passover. Jesus' arrival in Galilee—just in time, as it seemed—must have been eagerly grasped by the anxious father as the last hope for his sick son." [40] He came to Jesus and begged Him to come to where his child lay dying so Jesus could heal him. He made two assumptions in his approach to Jesus. First, he thought Jesus had to be physically present with his son to effect healing, and second, he did not realize that death did not limit the power of Jesus.

As Carson notes, this man was not interested in Christology, what Jesus was teaching, or probably even the kingdom of heaven. His only concern was the condition of his son and the fact that Jesus was reputed to be able to restore the infirm to health. Scripture reveals the royal official to have had a persistent manner as he continued to beseech Jesus. The boy had apparently been ill for a while, and his health was declining to the point of being close to death. This situation made the petition of the father more intense.

"There could be no more improbable scene in the world than an important court official hastening twenty miles to beg a favor from a village carpenter." [41] He was beyond caring what anyone thought or the possible ramifications for his duties under Herod Antipas. What mattered to him was the restoration of his son's health. Men in such positions as this official were "usually fastidious and haughty and did not willingly submit to being treated harshly. But it is worth noting that this man was humbled by his need and by his fear of losing his son; so he does not burst out in anger or grumble when Christ talks to him roughly, but allows the reproof to pass, keeping humbly quiet." [42]

The reply of Jesus seems harsh. "But it is addressed to a wider audience than the officer, as the plural 'you people' indicates. It is not so much Jesus' answer to the nobleman's request as a reflection He makes on the occasion of the request." [43] The implication of Jesus' rebuke to the crowd was that their desire to see a miracle or sign was not motivated by a desire to be drawn closer to God or to believe in Him, but more to marvel at the event. Jesus did not complain because the father sought a miracle to believe in Jesus; rather, the man had come to Him because he believed Jesus could perform healings. Jesus said, "Unless you people see signs and wonders, you simply will not believe."

This instance is the only time in the Fourth Gospel the word "wonders" describes the signs of Jesus. Borchert notes the reaction of Jesus is similar to His response to

His mother when she came to Him for help when the wedding party had exhausted the supply of wine. Keener echoes this observation and notes both the mother of Jesus and this official refused to accept the initial refusal of Jesus to provide assistance. The two incidents at this point diverge, with His mother accepting that Jesus was in charge and the royal official continuing to petition until Jesus took control of the situation and said to the man, "Go your way; your son lives."

In both instances, Jesus spoke and the person with whom He was talking obeyed. The man who sought Jesus had little concern or thought as to who Jesus was, but only for how He could satisfy his needs. Already in the ministry of Jesus, His ability to heal the sick and infirmed was overshadowing the real purpose of His ministry. The signs were necessary to validate His messianic claims, and they would continue in strength and intensity until the resurrection of Lazarus, but the majority of those who came to Jesus were seeking only miracles and solutions to their individual problems.

Despite Jesus' words, the nobleman continued to plead for his child. While the man did have some measure of faith, it was tenuous and weak; had Jesus refused to heal, his faith would have damaged or destroyed. To the credit of the pleading man, he did not defend or justify his petition but urged Jesus to intervene before his child died. How Jesus responded to the father is both surprising and demanding. Jesus said to the man, "Go your way; your son lives." The manner in which Jesus spoke of the child is significant, and this way of expressing the condition of the child is repeated later in the account.

Obviously, the royal official believed Jesus had to be in the physical presence of his young son to heal him, but now the healer had just told him to leave because his son lived. Both this man's understanding of the power of Jesus and his faith were considerably weaker than those of the centurion, for whom Jesus healed his slave, also at a distance. As a note, this character trait is hardly surprising since those in the military are more cognizant of authority, the hierarchy of command, and the requirements of delegation. However, for this man seeking help at this time and place, he had to take Jesus at His word, not knowing whether Jesus meant what He said about the health of the young child. The words of Jesus, rather than being consoling and helpful to the father, became a blunt and forceful challenge to make the man have faith.

The father was now in a quandary: would he accept the words of Jesus and depart not knowing whether his son lives, or would he continue to petition Jesus to come with him to where the young boy lay dying, thus taking the chance the words Jesus had just spoken might be revoked. The father accepts Jesus at His word and departed. In this situation, "Jesus was both demanding unquestioning faith in his word and promising the healing for which the man asked." [44]

Up to this point, the official's faith was based entirely on deeds or what he had seen or heard of the miracles and healings of Jesus. Now he was being compelled to believe only the words of Jesus, and without witnessing the deed. "The point of this story is that it illustrates a new dimension of believing; namely a believing without the immediacy of seeing. Accordingly, it foreshadows the concluding words of Thomas about believing without seeing (20:29)." [45] The conversation between the two men occurred during the seventh hour of the day.

Boice notes some similarities between this sign and the first. Both occurred on the "third day." In both instances, Jesus reprimanded the person making the request. When He performed the miracle, He only spoke without any further action. Finally, only servants in both instances were aware of the true nature of the events. The differences are obvious: one was a wedding with happiness and joy while the other was an illness with fear and death. There is some question of the time system John uses in this passage, but a brief analysis solves the problem. In the Jewish world, a day comprised the twelve hours from dawn to dusk with the day beginning around 6 'o clock in the morning. In the same way, the night was also twelve hours. The Roman day began at midnight and continued until the following midnight. However, typically it was legal establishment and the military that utilized this method of time keeping.

For everything else, the Romans, like the Jews, started the day at dawn. Roman sundials found by archeologists marking noon as VI rather than XII confirm this method of time-keeping. So, whether John used the Jewish or Roman method of telling time, the approximate time was one o'clock in the afternoon. "The father could have arrived home the same day. His confidence in the Lord, however, seems to have been so secure that he did not hurry.

Perhaps he was tired and hungry. Perhaps he stopped for rest and refreshment. There was no need for breakneck speed. All was well." [46] Thus, the man remained in Cana overnight and departed for home the next morning. On the way home, he met his slaves, who were coming to tell him the news of his son. When he inquired as to the health of the child, the servants explained the fever had broken at the seventh hour. The father knew this was the same time Jesus had told him his son lives, and, because of this sign, he and his household believed. With this sign, Jesus revealed to the disciples another aspect of His messianic claims.

CHAPTER SIX

THE THIRD TEACHING
THE DIVINE SON

JOHN 5:17-29

This teaching occurs after Jesus healed the man infirm for thirty-eight years. As you may recall, the passage tells of the beginning of the animosity between Jesus and the Pharisees and religious authorities, resulting in official persecution of Jesus. This teaching took place when the religious leaders questioned Jesus about His authority to heal and His penchant for healing on the Sabbath.

After Jesus had revealed His identity to the man when He found him in the Temple, the formerly crippled man went to the Pharisees to tell them the identity of his healer. Seemingly the most significant problem the religious leaders had with the healing was that it occurred on the Sabbath. This confrontation between Jesus and the religious leaders marked the beginning of the process that ultimately resulted in His trial and crucifixion.

The statements of Jesus in this passage were a legal response to the religious leaders who attacked His messianic claim from the legal or judicial perspective. The religious leaders sought to refute His seven messianic claims, for they threatened their perception of God and their place in Jewish society. Toward the end of the persecution of Jesus, the religious leaders also feared the uproar over Jesus would ultimately prompt Roman intervention.

This was the second set of charges brought against Jesus. The first set of charges (5:16) was that He was guilty of sin and of violating the Sabbath, punishable by public shaming. We find the defense of these charges in 5:30-47 and consists of witnesses testifying to the sinless acts of Jesus and His obedience. The second set of charges (5:18) were blasphemy and making Himself equal with God. Both of these charges were punishable by death. This passage contains the defense for these more severe charges.

The statement of Jesus that His Father was working until now and that He was working now is the first of several claims of deity in this passage, and His opponents instantly perceived His words in this manner.

To them what Jesus said was blasphemous, that He violated the Sabbath and was "making Himself equal with God." The religious leaders believed He was challenging the barrier between God and mortal, finite man. They felt this was contradictory to passages in the Old Testament where God asked who could be compared to Him. Those who made themselves like God were to be condemned as revealed in 2 Chronicles 24:24, Isaiah 14:13-15, and Ezekiel 28:2.

That Jesus healed a man inform thirty-eight years and had the temerity to instruct the healed man to carry his bedding in violation of Sabbath law was proof of how Jesus viewed Himself and, by implication, God. In the following verses, Jesus defended Himself and explained His relationship to the Father. While we frequently overlook these verses because they are difficult to understand, and they lack dramatic events, they are important because they contain seven statements of deity by Jesus along with an explanation of His messianic claims.

As Carson notes, if there was anything the Jews learned during the seventy-year exile, it was that idolatry was wrong, and God is holy. Now Jesus had made a claim that, to them, blatantly contradicted the bitter lessons from Babylon. The religious leaders sought to refute His words because of His claim to deity. It is important to understand the charge against Jesus and His response to the accusation. It is entirely possible the religious leaders did not properly listen to the words of Jesus; He never claimed to be God or to replace God, which was the essence of the charge against Him. Rather, He said God the Father sent him, He was doing the will of the Father, He was obedient to the Father, and He was bringing glory to the Father.

He was doing this as the Son of the Father; He watched and mimicked the actions of His Father. "It is significant that in the Fourth Gospel Jesus said either 'My Father' or 'your Father,' but never 'our Father.' God was His Father and also the Father of other men, but the Fatherhood of God meant more to Him than it did to others." [47] This passage contains two major points: the Son and His dependence on the Father (5:19-24) and the Son and Judgment (5:25-29). The Apostle John writes that Jesus answered the religious leaders, he also opens the statement of Jesus with a double amen or "truly, truly," which is a literary key in this Gospel denoting critical material.

Jesus said He did nothing of Himself, but all He did He saw the Father doing. He explained that whatever the Father did, He, the Son, did in like manner. He was "completely dependent upon the Father. In this expression of humility, obedience, and dependence, we see the Semitic version of the ideal son, since a son is to reproduce his father's thoughts and actions." [48] This passage is Jesus' second claim of deity, for He said He had done what the Father had done. By being perfectly obedient to the Father, Jesus acted in such a way as to reveal the Father, doing His deeds and obeying His will.

"Jesus rejects any idea that He would ascribe to Himself the authority and freedom that belongs only to God and thus put Himself next to God. He appeals to the fact that as Son He is not able to do anything of His own accord if He does not see the Father do it." [49]

He was not acting independently of the Father because He could not act independently of the Father. "This very relationship of the Son to the Father makes it simply impossible that Jesus should do anything 'of Himself,' so that the thing would emanate from Him alone and be done by Him alone, separate and apart from the Father, and thus deviating from and contradictory to the Father's will—even as the Jews charged that Jesus was breaking God's Sabbath law." [50] He defended His actions on the Sabbath on the basis of following the will of the Father. The theme of the dependence of Jesus on the Father permeates the Fourth Gospel as seen in John 3:34, 8:26, 8:42, 9:4, and 12:49.

Jesus saw the Father work on the Sabbath; thus, following the example of God, He healed on the Sabbath. Did God keep the Sabbath law? If He did not, He was a law-breaker, and this was an unacceptable conclusion. However, if God did not work on the Sabbath, then who keeps the universe orderly? Because of the logic of this reasoning, rabbis were in general agreement that God did work on the Sabbath; since His domain was everywhere, He was not in violation of Sabbath law because His "house" was the universe. Nothing was too high, too low, or too far, because wherever God went He was within His abode; and, therefore, He was not a law-breaker.

After stating He could do nothing of Himself except what He saw the Father doing and was also doing what the Father did, Jesus added "in like manner," which further solidified His claim of deity and His relationship to the Father. The second part of verse nineteen beginning with "for" is an inclusion statement that continues through verse twenty-three. In these few verses, Jesus said "for" four times, which indicates the structure and unity of thought in these verses. Jesus revealed He was in no way inferior to the Father, because He, Jesus, fulfilled the redemptive plan of the Father in the incarnate condition. As a human being, Jesus kept His eye on the Father and was thus able to act as the Father even in a human body.

The thought continues in verse twenty, shown by the second "for," where He explained the relationship between Himself and the Father. The Father loved the Son with a never-ending love. In the same way, the Son loved the Father and sought to emulate Him in every way. This love gave and never held back; thus, the Father had shown and was now showing, past and present tense, the Son all He did. This passage implies the Son had done and was doing, both past and present tense, everything He witnessed of the Father. This incident is the third proof of deity: Jesus could see all things the Father did, which made Him equal to the Father.

This statement does not limit or imply the power and ability of Jesus. Rather, Jesus never sought His will, but the will of His Father. Jesus never acted independently of the Father. There were perfect unity and singleness of purpose between the two. This unity and singleness of purpose imply the actions of Jesus were God-based rather than human. For this reason, He was always in the will of the Father and would, therefore, accomplish greater works and greater things. During the remainder of His ministry, His signs increased in power, proving the words He spoke in this confrontation were true. As the next few verses reveal, Jesus claimed the authority through His relationship with the Father to also give life and to judge. As the Son acted in response to the Father, He revealed the Father by doing His will, and this also demonstrated the Father's love for the Son.

Some scholars suggest Jesus used His relationship with the Father as an illustration. In the same manner, a young man receives training in his father's trade or vocation, Jesus watched and learned from His Father. Many in the audience could have understood this because this was the usual manner of education for Jewish children at the time of Jesus. A five- or six-year-old child would start Beth Sefer (elementary school) and continue to about the age of twelve. The girls would return home where their mothers continued their education. Boys who demonstrated potential would continue their formal education while the majority would return home for an apprenticeship in the father's occupation. "In a simple society like that of Palestine, a trade would be taught within a family, and the son would have to imitate the father's work." [51] In the same manner, Jesus said He imitated His Father. Like any analogy or parable, this conveyed a basic concept, and we should not overanalyze every nuance. Intense scrutiny of every facet of this or any illustration or parable in Scripture can cause unforeseen problems; use these vignettes as aids to understanding the spiritual message within the verses.

The third repetition of the word "for" in verse twenty-one indicates the continuity of thought. The Son did what He saw the Father doing: resurrecting people from spiritual death and giving them life. That Jesus was able, like the Father, to resurrect the spiritually dead was the fourth claim to deity Jesus spoke in this passage. That the Father gives spiritual life is solidly grounded in the Old Testament. Deuteronomy 32:39, 1 Samuel 2:6, and 2 Kings 5:7 affirm this point: Judaism readily accepted the concept of God possessing this authority and power. Here Jesus began to enunciate the authority He possessed and clarified the ramifications of His authority. Jesus claimed, because of His dependence on the Father, He also had the divine prerogative to give life to whomever He chose. This divine perogative was probably the most significant power spoke by Jesus: the power to give life. The healing of the man infirmed thirty-eight years while bypassing many other infirm people was a visual explanation of this authority.

Now that Jesus established His relationship with the Father, He continued the thought by revealing that, to ensure He would receive the same honor as God the Father, the authority to judge had been given to Him. "One cannot honor the Father without honoring the Son; the honor of the Father and the Son is identical; in the Son we are confronted by the Father and we can approach the Father only through the Son." [52] It is important to note this statement in verse twenty-two begins with "for," and this was the fourth time Jesus spoke the word in four verses. The construction ties together the thought of these four verses.

This statement was the fifth claim of deity Jesus spoke, and the Jews took His words in this manner. The Jews believed they would stand before God for judgment. Jewish doctrine taught the judgment on the last day was one of the most sovereign acts of God. He had judged in the past, both the Chosen People and the peoples surrounding the Jews, but Jesus was saying that at the final judgment they would appear before Him. That the Father would give this role to Jesus was anathema to the Jews. This delegation did not diminish God because the glorification of the Son honored the Father. The unspoken message, of course, in this statement was that anyone who dishonored the Son also dishonored the Father, which put the religious leaders in a difficult position.

Jesus repeated the double amen, "truly, truly," and explained how the relationship between Himself and the Father also impacted how people are saved. Anyone who heard His (Jesus) word and believed Him (God) who sent Him (Jesus) would be saved. In this context, most scholars believe "word" means the entirety of His teachings. The believer immediately moves from the position of awaiting judgment into a state of eternal life. This statement likely reminded the religious leaders of the instantaneous healing of the man infirm thirty-eight years. In the same way, Jesus portrayed judgment as immediate, and the one judged received either an acquittal or condemnation. This portrayal contrasted with the Jewish view of judgment at the end of the Age; instead, those who rejected Jesus were judged here and now. To believe in Jesus now means eternal life now and forever. The double amen forms an inclusion statement with the double amen of verse nineteen; we should view everything in this passage as a single theological entity.

The second component of the words of Jesus dealt with judgment. The preceding passage explains the Father had given Him this authority. In verse twenty-five, Jesus spoke the double amen, "truly, truly," and explained that now the dead would hear His voice. This happening is the sixth claim to deity Jesus spoke in this passage. Jesus was speaking of the physically dead, not spiritually dead. Jesus revealed that not only did He have power given to Him by the Father over the living, but He also had power over death. He had already shown His power in several signs. His voice to raise the dead was the voice of God, for God had the power of life and death. At this point in His ministry, Jesus had yet to resurrect anyone from the dead, but He later raised the son of a widow (Luke 7:11-17), the daughter of Jairus (Luke 8:41-46). At the end of His ministry, Lazarus (John 11:1-44) who had been dead for four days. This event confirmed His claims to the religious leaders of His true identity and relationship with the Father. This passage is one of only three times Jesus referred to Himself as the Son of God. The other occasions are John 10:36 and John 19:7.

Jesus then affirmed that the Father breathed life into people and life was the Father's gift and God was the fountain of life as confirmed by Genesis 2:7, Job 10:12, and Psalm 36:9. Jesus had the same kind of life the Father had; like the Father, Jesus possessed the gift of life. "Most importantly, God gives Jesus the greatest of God's powers, namely the eschatological power to raise the dead, judge them, and requite them. All of this, moreover, is God's grant or gift to Jesus." [53] For this reason, the Father has given us eternal life, and that life is in the Son. God is the judge of the earth, and we see this role throughout the Old Testament including Genesis 18:25 and Judges 11:27. The Jews would have well received this statement.

At this point in the passage, the three concepts join. First, as the Son of God, Jesus had the authority to execute judgment just as the Father, which is the seventh claim of deity Jesus spoke in this confrontation. This statement reiterated His equality with the Father and authority from the Father. Second, Jesus was the one to whom all authority had been given and whose kingdom would endure forever. Third, by being human, He knew our frailties and weaknesses and was thus qualified to be a judge because He knew our condition. This statement connects the divinity of Jesus with the humanity of Jesus and makes Him uniquely qualified to judge for an everlasting kingdom. Those who reject Him are already judged, and those who accept Him have already passed from judgment into eternal life.

In verses twenty-eight and twenty-nine, Jesus reached a climax in defense of His sovereignty and tied together the two premises of His response to the Pharisees: the unity He had with the Father and His right to judge, which defined His unity with the Father. He revealed that He would call the dead from the grave; not only did Jesus possess the requisite authority from the Father to judge now, but also the divine authority to judge the dead later. Judgment will be at the end of the Age, but those alive who rejects the Messiah are condemned. Those who are alive today and believe pass from judgment and have eternal life. For those who are presently dead, at a future time, Jesus will return and call them to judgment. Their judgment will be based on works, and those who have done good deeds will rise to live while those who have done evil will be condemned.

Tenney offers the following comparison showing this relationship between the Father and Son.

The Father has a special relationship with Son (5:17).
The Son is dependent on Father (5:19).

The Father originates the works of the Son (5:19).
The Son has perfect knowledge of Father (5:20).

The Father loves the Son (5:20).
The Son possesses life (5:21).

The Father shows the Son His works (5:20).
The Son is equal in honor with Father (5:23).

The Father gives judgment of men to the Son (5:22, 27).
The Son raises the dead (5:25, 28).

The Father receives the worship of man (5:23).
The Son is the means of salvation (5:24).

The Father possesses inherent life (5:26).
The Father endows Son with inherent life (5:26).

CHAPTER SEVEN

THE THIRD SIGN
HEALING THE MAN CRIPPLED 38 YEARS

JOHN 5:1-18

The third sign, the healing of the man crippled thirty-eight years, revealed another aspect of the divinity and power of Jesus: His authority over time. He had been ministering in Galilee but travelled with His disciples to Jerusalem to celebrate the Jewish feasts. As with first two signs, this sign added more validity or authenticity to His messianic claims. There seem to be two reasons John includes this sign in the Fourth Gospel. "First, it was this miracle that marked the beginning of angry disbelief and hostility toward Jesus on the part of the Jewish leaders. It is to this theme the Gospel now turns.

Second, there is also the fact that this story illustrates how Jesus came to the weak and helpless and saved them." [54] As many scholars have noted, the expression "after these things" is a preferred literary technique of John to refer to an indeterminate period, and the material he is writing about is not in the synoptic Gospels but supplements them. When this chapter opens, the Galilean ministry was concluded, and Jesus and the disciples were in Jerusalem celebrating a feast, the name of which is unknown.

Judaism celebrated three feasts in which Jews who lived within fifteen miles of Jerusalem were expected to attend at the Temple: Passover, Pentecost, and the Tabernacles. Of course, many pilgrims came from much further away; for some, it was a once-in-a-lifetime journey. While a consensus is lacking as to the identity of the feast, most scholars believe the event was either the Feast of the Tabernacles or Pentecost. Schnackenburg notes that Pentecost nicely fits a timeline of the Feast of Tabernacles in chapter seven, the Feast of Dedication in chapter nine, and the last Passover in chapters eleven and twelve. Jesus and His disciples were in Jerusalem for the first Passover. He first cleared out the Temple then left and travelled to Galilee where He spent an indeterminate period, during which He healed Peter's mother and the royal official's son.

As Blomberg notes, it is "exactly what we should expect, that Jesus, a faithful Jew, should join the Galilean throngs in Jerusalem during the various festivals mandated by Mosaic Law. Nothing in either John or the Synoptic Gospels suggest that Jesus ever violated the written Law; His conflicts revolved around the 'oral Torah'" [55] This helps explain the seemingly disjointed narrative of several chapters in the Fourth Gospel that has Jesus going back and forth between Jerusalem and Galilee. Jesus came to Jerusalem to celebrate the unidentified feast and heal the man crippled thirty-eight years only to be confronted by the Pharisees, which marked the start of the persecution, and returned to Galilee.

This account is interesting for several reasons. According to Neyrey, this passage is a healing narrative typical of the time and place from both Hellenistic and Jewish tradition. "Such stories typically contained five elements: confrontation, the severity of disease, cure, sometimes with material medios (such as roots or spittle), proof of healing, and honor to the healer." [56] While there was an interaction between Jesus and the person He healed on a one-to-one basis; the roles seem reversed in the sense that Jesus approached the person needing assistance instead of the person coming to Him.

There appears to have been no effort by Jesus to gauge or require faith before the healing. Despite this seeming reversal, John's Gospel "stresses both divine sovereignty and human responsibility, and here we see both Jesus' sovereign approach to this man and the importance of the man's own will." [57] There is also the introduction of the expanding influence of the actions of Jesus in the sense that the Fourth Gospel introduces the Pharisees and religious leaders as antagonists to Jesus.

In many ways, this sign was a bridge taking Him from the rural setting of Galilee and their acceptance to the conflicts and challenges in Jerusalem. Jesus is healing on the Sabbath only intensified the conflict with the Pharisees and religious leaders. Tracing the path Jesus took to Jerusalem, He went south from Galilee through Samaria into Judea. Upon arriving in Jerusalem, He passed through an entrance on the north side called the Sheep's Gate. Nehemiah 3:1 provides information about this place.

Other mentions include Nehemiah 3:52 and 12:38-39. Sheep were brought to the Temple for sacrifices through this gate. "In Jesus' day, this apparently was a small opening in the north wall of the temple. The sheep were washed in the pool before being taken to the sanctuary. This was also the place where invalids lay in the hope of being healed." [58] If Jesus and His disciples came from Galilee, it would make sense they would take advantage of this entrance to the city.

The Aramaic name for where the invalids lay is uncertain. It could have been Bethsaida, Bethesda, or Bethzatha; all of these variations are feasible. The Copper Scroll found at Quran provides strong support for the structure itself and the expression of Bethesda or the house of outpouring. Also, the original language means twin or double pools. The Copper Scroll, along with the identifying feature of five colonnades or porches, provides sufficient confirmation that the pool where the third sign took place was, in fact, Bethesda.

Each pool was about the size of a football field with the north pool being slightly smaller than the other, and both pools about twenty feet deep. A porch was on each of the four sides of the double pools with the fifth porch across the center between the two pools, a space of about twenty feet. It was similar to hot springs or healing spas of today. Archeologists discovered the double pools in 1888 in conjunction with repairs to the Church of St. Anne, which is located at St. Stephen's gate in Jerusalem. Facilities such as this were public places during the time of Jesus, and beggars and the infirm were frequent visitors.

Lenski notes the passage lists four types of individuals who were at the pools—sick, blind, lame, and withered. In Scripture the number four means completeness, and the listing of the four types without articles between the nouns emphasizes the ailments and the allusion to four. The fourth verse of the chapter tells of an angel stirring the water and the healing of the first person to enter the water. This verse is not in the earliest manuscripts; the most likely source is gloss.

The source of water to the pools was Solomon's pools, located southwest of Bethlehem. An underground spring fed water into Solomon's pool and intermittently caused disturbances. Whatever the reason and the one parenthetically given in this passage is as good as any, people desperate for healing came to Bethesda. It is unknown whether the stirred water ever cured anyone, but enough people believed, according to the passage, that a multitude came to the pool. This was why the man who had been infirm for thirty-eight years was there. As Dodd notes, in this narrative, like the water in the stone pots at the wedding in Cana, there is "once again, water that offers healing (or newness of life), but has not been effective to heal a cripple of thirty-eight years' standing." [59]

When Jesus came to the pool, He approached the man and asked whether he wanted to get well. The passage does not explain how Jesus knew of the man's condition or how long he had been infirmed. Some translations imply Jesus could have gained this information by asking questions, but the prevailing assumption is that Jesus possessed divine knowledge of the man, his infirmities, and his sins. We should not view the question as psychological in nature, but to ask if the man sought to be healed. As with most of the other signs, Jesus took the initiative of the encounter.

Obviously, the man did not know with whom he was speaking, for he responded that, while he sought to get well, his condition prevented him from getting into the water before anyone else. The focus of the man was the promise of the pool, not the man speaking to him. "The man had waited for thirty-eight years, and it might well have been that hope had died and left behind a passive and dull despair. In his heart of hearts, the man might be well content to remain an invalid for, if he were healed, he would have to shoulder all the burden of making a living." [60]

Notice the man implied blame for circumstances seemingly beyond his control; he did not seek the name of his benefactor, and he implicated Jesus when the Pharisees asked why he was carrying his pallet on the Sabbath. These three facts indicate this individual was of dubious character. The picture John creates in just a few verses is one of an individual interested only in himself. Phillips notes the action of Jesus to heal the man on the Sabbath was purposeful and meant to challenge the religious authorities and tradition.

Some interpret this passage as an allegory, but it would be more accurate to apply the hermeneutic method used at the time of the writing—a four-level interpretation of p'shat, remez, d'rash, and sod. The basic premise of the message behind the word is the supremacy of Jesus and the failure of Judaism. The thirty-eight years are interesting since that was the period the Israelites wandered the Wilderness before entering the Promised Land, which is likely a hint or remez to Deuteronomy 2;14.

Wiersbe suggests the Apostle John "saw in this a picture of his Jewish nation that had wandered in the wilderness for thirty-eight years. Spiritually speaking, Israel was a nation of impotent people, waiting hopelessly for something to happen." [61] Haenchen notes "it is scarcely too bold to interpret the story as follows: the sick man, whom Jesus restores to free movement and health after thirty-eight years of immobility and who does not thank Jesus for it but makes common cause with the disciples of Moses against Jesus, is the embodiment of law-bound Judaism, in the same way as the Samaritan woman represents the Samaritan people and religion." [62]

Another hint or remez to the Old Testament is that the five porches around the pools represent the five books of the Torah, but the Judaic religion could not heal spiritually, just as it was not possible, apart from Jesus, to heal physically. The occasional stirring of the water uses the same language as the Psalm, which speaks of the Exodus. The fact the man ultimately chose to remain in the Judaic faith is also interpreted as a portrayal of those Jews who rejected the message and signs of Jesus inaugurating the kingdom. Another remez to the Old Testament is that the movement of the water represents baptism. The matching of the years of the man's crippled condition to the length of the time in the Wilderness and the five porches relating to the five books of the Torah may be coincidental, but these could all be elements of the hermeneutical methodology used by Jesus and His contemporaries.

Upon hearing the crippled man's reply, Jesus instructed him to arise, take up his pallet and walk. Instantly the man was healed, despite not knowing the name of his benefactor and with no manifestation of faith, no indication of repentance, and seemingly no recognition of Jesus. He rose to his feet, picked up his pallet, and walked away. Another element of this miracle is sometimes overlooked: "when a man has not walked for a long time he must learn again, and this man needed not to learn. His muscles were firm, and responded to his will as if perfectly trained and practiced." [63] Of all the signs, this one is probably the most bizarre as the man did not seek to know the name of the man who healed him and did not thank or worship the person who healed him but walked away carrying his bedding. With all attention on the healed man, Jesus slipped away anonymously into the crowd. At this point, the man did not know the identity of his benefactor, but this would soon change.

The healing occurred on the Sabbath, and the man was breaking Sabbath law by carrying his bedding. The Pharisees confronted the man demanding a reason for his carrying a pallet. The Pharisees may have been willing to accommodate violation of the Oral Law or the Traditions in some aspects, but when it came to the Sabbath, they were uncompromising. The Law, concerning the Sabbath, had been defined to the minutest degree, and any violation merited an immediate response. The basis for the accusation comes from several Old Testament passages such as Exodus 20:9-10, Nehemiah 13:15-19, and Jeremiah 17:19-27.

According to the rabbis, there were thirty-nine types of work forbidden on the Sabbath. These included sowing, plowing, reaping, binding (sheaves), threshing, winnowing, cleaning crops, grinding, sifting, kneading, baking, preparing, shearing, washing, beating, or dying, spinning, weaving, weaving or separating two threads, tying, loosening, and sewing or tearing to sew. It also included hunting, slaughtering, flaying, salting or curing of animal skin, scraping or cutting of animal skin, writing two letters, erasing to write two letters, constructing, tearing down, lighting or extinguishing a fire, striking with a hammer, taking from one domain to another.

Upon questioning, the man replied that the man who had healed him told him to pick up the pallet and walk. The Pharisees asked the identity of who had given the order to violate the law. It is revealing the Pharisees would ask the identity of who induced the violation of the Sabbath rather than who had healed. The man professed ignorance of his benefactor. The man was permitted to depart, for the Pharisees were seemingly less concerned about one individual breaking the Sabbath law than the person encouraging the violation of the law.

At some point later, and the Gospel account does not specify the length of time, Jesus accosted the man in the Temple, which was just south of the pools. It is probably safe to assume, based on the wording of the passage that this second meeting occurred later the same day, but it is possible this meeting occurred several days later. Whenever it happened, Jesus found the man whom He had healed in the Temple and noted he was well again but warned him, if he did not stop sinning, something worse might happen to him.

This conversation contains some interesting points and also raises several questions. The man, though infirm for many years, was apparently of good health before becoming infirm. He was old enough to remember he had been well because Jesus had implied this fact. This suggests the man's age to be near fifty, but it is impossible to determine with any more accuracy. Most people remember little before the age of ten, so if he were twelve when he became infirm, the thirty-eight years would make him fifty. If, for example, he had been in his late teens or early twenties—say twenty-two—when he became infirm, his age would be around sixty. The way Jesus spoke to the man also reveals He knew the sin to which He was referring and the formerly ill man knew full well that Jesus knew.

The tenses of the words Jesus speaks suggest the man had been and was continuing to sin, and Jesus was warning of the consequences. The present tense of the words Jesus spoke indicates the current condition of the man, not what happened some thirty-eight years previously. We should note there is no word spoken by

Jesus or written by the Apostle John suggesting sin caused the man's condition. This phrasing is consistent with the words of Jesus when He healed the man born blind that neither his sins nor those of his parents caused his blindness. Over the centuries, there has been much conjecture about this encounter between Jesus and the healed man, but many apply a false or overly speculative interpretation and use the words of Jesus with less than honorable intentions.

Apparently, the healing and words Jesus spoke failed to generate faith in the man. The religious leaders had questioned the man as to the reason he was carrying his pallet, but when he returned to report who his benefactor was, the man said it had been Jesus who healed him rather than who told him to carry his pallet. It does not seem the man was trying "to get Jesus into trouble, but the actual words of the law were: 'If anyone carries anything from a public place to a private house on the Sabbath intentionally he is punishable by death by stoning.' He was simply trying to explain that it was not his fault that he had broken the law." [64] As Bock notes, technically Jesus did not violate the Sabbath commandment against carrying a load, but He induced another to be in violation of the regulation. The Pharisees then asked the man what had happened—though they already knew—to obtain testimony for legal action against Jesus. With this man's testimony in hand, the Pharisees confronted Jesus because He had healed on the Sabbath.

This healing marked the beginning of the official persecution of Jesus by the religious leaders and signaled a dramatic shift in the manner in which the religious leaders viewed Jesus. What could have exacerbated the situation was a change in Roman dealings with the Jewish nation. "The anti-Semite Roman commander, Sejanus, working through Pilate, deprived the Sanhedrin, the ruling body of the Jewish nation, of its jurisdiction over capital crimes, with the result that the Sanhedrin had to abandon the Great Hall of Hewn Stone in the Temple court and move as a body to the market of Annas on the temple mount. We see the results of this change a year or so later when the Sanhedrin was compelled to come to Pilate seeking the death penalty, in the case of Jesus." [65] This new level of harshness could have proven fertile ground for rebellion or revolt, which would have further damaged the position of the religious leaders.

Because of the deteriorating situation in Rome, they were more aware of possible troublemakers who could bring unwanted attention from the occupying forces. This conflict between Jesus and His detractors continued until His eventual trial and crucifixion. In reality, the religious leaders were well within their scope of responsibilities to investigate new teachers to verify that their message was not heretical or false. John the Baptist had undergone the same scrutiny (John 1:19-27) and the religious leaders were in the process of investigating Jesus. For this healing of the man crippled for thirty-eight years to provoke such a strong response suggests previous Sabbath healings by Jesus and other transgressions that had offended Pharisaic sensibilities. The understanding of the Sabbath held by the religious leaders was erroneous. "The Sabbath was not merely a rule for humans but a gift to humans. It was to be used to honor God and to benefit his people. More importantly, Jesus was Lord of the Sabbath." [66]

The reply of Jesus to the religious leaders, "My Father is working until now, and I Myself am working," contains several meanings. "The implications of this argument were immediately apparent is witnessed by the violence of the reaction. For the Jews, the Sabbath privilege was peculiar to God, and no one was equal to God." [67] The first statement that the Father was working until now is the major premise and reveals the degree of activity of God in the world and the dependence of the world on the Father. If the Father were not working, as Jesus pointed out, there would be chaos. God working on the Sabbath was accepted by the rabbis, as it was evident that He did work on the seventh day.

One of the arguments of the rabbis to justify God working on the Sabbath was that Exodus 20:11 and Deuteronomy 5:15 commanded a man not to carry a burden outside his dwelling. Isaiah 6:3 reveals the whole world is full of His glory meaning the dwelling of God was everywhere[thus this prohibition was not violated. Another Sabbath law was that a man could not carry a distance of his height, but Jeremiah 23:24

reveals God fills both heaven and earth. Thus, He could not violate this Sabbath law. It is noteworthy Jesus uses the term "My Father," whereas the Jews did not refer to God in such an intimate manner.

The subordinate component of Jesus' argument that He was also working "indicated that He made the Father His pattern, and the He felt that the Father's work constituted sufficient precedent and reason for His." [68] The religious leaders are aware of the argument. Also, the manner in which Jesus spoke the statement also indicated He was equal to the Father, which was abhorrent to the sensibilities of the Pharisees. In this confrontation, Jesus not only rebuked His critics for criticizing His working on the Sabbath but claimed to be equal to the Father, directly challenging the Pharisaic position of the relationship between God and man.

CHAPTER EIGHT

THE FOURTH TEACHING
THE BREAD OF LIFE

JOHN 6:26-58

In this teaching, Jesus took something familiar to His audience—bread—and applied a new spiritual concept in a powerful and unforgettable way. Bread, being a staple at the time of Jesus, was a perfect vehicle to implement an eternal spiritual truth. Rabbinical teaching used the same technique, so Jesus was able to take the familiar to introduce a new concept.

This teaching took place at Capernaum, the base of His Galilean mission. Jesus had just returned to the western side of the Sea of Galilee following the feeding of the five thousand and walking on the water. Once the crowds, who had been on the other side of the lake, realized where Jesus was, they came by boat also to Capernaum. When they found Him, the city being rather small, they asked when He had come back, as they had all been watching for Him and the last time they knew of His location, it was on the other side of the Sea of Galilee. In all likelihood, they were still intent on making Him a king.

Jesus ignored the question of He came to be in Capernaum. Rather, He opened with the double amen or "truly, truly" and told them they were seeking Him because they had been fed, not for the meaning of the sign. He then took the physical food He had provided and transitioned the topic to spiritual food. Jesus told the crowd to not work for the food that perishes, but for the food that leads to eternal life. This statement is d'rash or spiritual in that He took the physical and applied to it a spiritual meaning or application.

Naturally enough, the crowd, quickly understanding the metaphor, asked Him how they could obtain eternal life. In response, He used the recent sign of His feeding of the five thousand to explain the kingdom of heaven. Much of the dialog is strikingly parallel to the conversation of Jesus with the Samaritan woman at the Sychar well about water. It is important to note that Jesus substituted the plural "works of God" with the singular "work of God." In doing so, He made a single thing obvious: faith. Instead of works, as the Law stipulates, the Jews had to believe in Him.

The Jews may have initially understood the food that leads to eternal life to refer to the Law when they asked what they must do. They were focused on works they should perform, which was not surprising given the basis of the Judaic religion. They believed that in seeking blessings from God they had to perform new works, and they wanted to know from Jesus what works they had to accomplish. As Morris notes, the present subjunctive verb form meant they were continuing to ask Jesus. This relationship between works and belief is crucial in the Fourth Gospel and the dynamic between the two can be seen several times in the Gospel of John.

The response of Jesus in verse twenty-nine is "nothing less than stunning: God's requirements are summed up as believing 'in the one He has sent,' that is, the Messiah." [69] The people, in contrast, were focused on the Law and what God required of them and did not recognize Jesus as introducing a new relationship with God. They were still confident they could perform works to meet the requirements of God. Note the verb tenses of the crowd's question and Jesus' response. They asked Him what works, in the plural form, they should perform, and Jesus corrected them and spoke of the work, in the singular form, which was to believe in Him as the Messiah. The change in verb tense is striking.

The crowd, upon hearing they should not work for food that perishes but for the food that endures to eternal life, asked Jesus for a sign. This request seemed to be a reference to the manna provided by Jesus, but the problem is that Jesus had just presented a sign that was very similar to this request. A possible explanation of this seeming repetition of a request for a sign is that this was a different group of people than the multitude of 5,000. At this point in the discussion, the underlying theme was the manna given to the Israelites during their time in the Wilderness.

That the time of year was very near the Passover only intensified the recollection of Moses and the manna. "The challenge to Jesus to produce manna or its equivalent as a sign is quite understandable if they thought of Him as the Prophet-like Moses." [70] Despite the fact that He miraculously fed 12,000 to 15,000 persons and presumably despite other signs (verse twenty-six), they were expecting greater signs since Jesus was greater than Moses. That these people demanded a sign revealed them to be unbelieving and unwilling to accept Jesus or His messianic claims. "Despite seeing signs, some refuse to believe, and others, while valuing the signs, fail to see beyond them to that which they signify." [71] As Keener observes, people are known to listen to well-known speakers with the goal of entertainment but with no intention of change.

It is likely the crowd had not grasped what Jesus had said and was fixated on a physical manifestation of a kingdom. Just on the other side of the Sea of Galilee, He had miraculously provided bread enough for a multitude to be filled and the crowd associated the sign with an expectation that when the Messiah came, He would provide manna just as Moses had done. According to Jewish belief, "the renewal of manna becomes a fixed feature of Jewish eschatological expectations.

We may, therefore, take it that the Jews here are represented as demanding that Jesus shall establish His messianic pretensions by the well-recognized token of restoring the gift of manna." [72] What Jesus had done in feeding the multitude and in the earlier signs, they interpreted as indicators of a physical kingdom complete with bread and water, just as God gave the Israelites during their forty years in the Wilderness. They even quoted Nehemiah 9:15, Psalm 78:24, and 205:40 as the promise of bread out of heaven to eat.

Jesus responded with a double amen, or "truly, truly," to signify the importance of what He was about to say. In actuality, this portion of the passage comprises a rabbinical debate, a common form of teaching at the time, between Jesus and His opponents. The basis of this debate was the giving of manna to the Israelites by Moses. The crowd was focused on the manna Moses supposedly gave them, and they sought the same type of sign from Jesus. The basis of their position was most likely Exodus chapter sixteen, as it mentions bread and the grumbling by the Israelites. Jesus used the same concept of bread but applied a new meaning: Him being the true bread from heaven. Jesus had to correct their misconceptions about Moses and the true source of the manna. "Moses was an instrument in God's hands, and he would be the first one to repudiate the use they were making of his name." [73]

God, not Moses, gave the manna to the Israelites during their wanderings in the Wilderness. To turn their attention from Moses and manna, Jesus explained that "My Father," which may or may not have been noticed by His audience, gave the true bread from heaven, alluding to Himself. Using difference tenses to make His point, "Jesus bridges Israel's past to the present by moving from the past tense in 6:32 to the present one in 6:33." [74] Neyrey details the six points of conflict between Jesus and the Jews.

Claim of the Jews	**Challenge of Jesus**
(1) Moses	**(1)** Not Moses, but My Father
(2) gave	**(2)** gives
(3) them	**(3)** you
(4) bread	**(4)** true bread
(5) from heaven	**(5)** from heaven
(6) to eat.	**(6)** to eat.

Schnackenburg points out the similarities between verses 32-35 and 48-51.

Negative condition

Verse 32 "It is not Moses who has given you the bread out of heaven, but it is My Father who gives you the true bread out of heaven."

Verse 49 "Your fathers ate the manna in the wilderness, and they died."

Definition
Verse 33 "For the bread of God is that which comes down out of heaven, and gives life to the world."
Verse 50 "This is the bread that comes down out of heaven so that one may eat of it and not die."

Self-introduction
Verse 35a "I am the bread of life..."
Verse 51a "I am the living bread that came down out of heaven; if one eats of this bread, he shall live forever, and the bread also that I shall give for the life of the world is My flesh..."

Demand
Verse 35b, c "...he who comes to Me shall not hunger, and he who believes in Me..."
Verse 51b "I am the living bread that came down out of heaven; if one eats..."

Promise
Verse 35b, c "...shall not hunger, shall never thirst."
Verse 51b "...he shall live forever."

Jesus used a typical rabbinical style of teaching in this run-in with the Jews in that He corrected their interpretation of Scripture and explained the true meaning of the words in the Old Testament and how the true bread was not from Moses but God. He continued to talk about the true bread, speaking on the d'rash or spiritual level that it came from heaven and gave life to the whole world. The people perceived on the plain or p'shat level and failed to understand that Jesus was communicating on the d'rash or spiritual level.

It is also interesting to note the Apostle John "employs a linguistic device that is not accessible to us in English. The word for bread in Greek is masculine in gender. As a consequence, 'that which comes down from heaven' can be taken to refer either to 'bread' or Jesus in Greek." [75] Here is another example of Johannine writing using double meanings or play or words. Not fully understanding what Jesus was saying, "the crowd wants an unending supply of this bread, perhaps like the Samaritan woman sought an unending supply of water so she would not have to go to the well again. Once the crowd realizes He is referring to Himself, however, they become far less receptive." [76] The crowd, like the Samaritan woman, missed the meaning because they were listening at the wrong level.

Jesus tried to explain the differences between manna and the bread He offered. He said to the crowd that He was the bread of life and whoever came to Him would never hunger or thirst. Again, He was speaking on the d'rash or spiritual level, and again the crowd refused to understand, for He immediately told the crowd they did not believe, even though they had seen Him. There would be no sign; He was the sign, yet they did not perceive. Those in the crowd who sought to make Jesus a king were not true followers because they failed to understand His purpose and mission. They were thinking on the physical or p'shat level, whereas Jesus had spoken in this entire encounter almost exclusively on the spiritual or d'rash level.

Jesus gave an in-depth explanation of His purpose and His relationship with the Father. He further explained He was submissive to the will of the Father, and it was the Father's will that of all whom He had given Jesus, none would be lost, but they would all be resurrected on the last day. He summarized His statement in verse forty: it was the will of the Father that everyone who believes in the Son has eternal life and that He, Jesus, will resurrect those persons on the last day. The purpose of Jesus was not that everyone who witnesses signs would come to believe in Him, but that He was following the will of the Father. Those whom the Father brought to faith in Jesus, He would welcome and preserve, again following the will of the Father.

Morris notes the work of salvation is a perfect harmony between Jesus and the Father. He came to earth to do the will of the Father, and these verses are a perfect summation of the Father's will. For this reason, Jesus was sent. This chapter mentions His coming down from heaven seven times (6:33, 38, 41, 42, 60, 51, and 58), and the number seven, in Scripture, indicates perfection.

The Jews—and it interesting that the Apostle John introduces this term here—grumbled and did not like Jesus' words. There may have been a break in the action at this point. They were in a different location; Jesus first talked to the crowd, predominately rural Galileans, where they found Him, but the conversation may have moved to the synagogue where better-schooled Galileans were present in greater number, which would have meant that opposition to Jesus would have been more concentrated.

Kostenberger and Borchert, among others, note the grumbling was identical to the grumbling of the Israelites toward Moses during their years in the wilderness. The Jews grumbled at the first bread, or manna, from heaven; now they were grumbling at the second bread, the true meaning of what the first bread represented, from heaven.

It is entirely possible that Apostle John is making this very point, that the attitude of those Jews who opposed Jesus was the same as those who opposed Moses during the forty years of the wilderness. It is not so much that the crowd's religious composition was Jewish; virtually all of the people with whom Jesus interacted were of the Jewish faith, and when He interacted with someone who was not Jewish, the Fourth Gospel emphatically points out the religious or cultural identity of the individual.

The designation of the Fourth Gospel to the "Jews," therefore, likely points to the attitude of those who grumbled against Moses and, generations later, grumbled against Jesus. Regardless of where Jesus ministered, those grumblers were present. In

Jerusalem, the opposition came because He made statements they took to mean that He was making Himself equal to the Father. Now opposition had risen among the grumblers in Galilee because they "knew" the identity of Jesus to be the son of Mary and Joseph. "There is irony here, for 'the Jews' were sure they knew Jesus' origins, but the reader of the Gospel knows differently. The Prologue says that Jesus is the Logos become flesh," [77] and Matthew, Mark, and Luke explain that, though Jesus was supposedly the son of Joseph, He was really the Son of God. They just knew the claim of Jesus was false and chose to focus almost exclusively on His claim of being sent from heaven.

In verses forty-three and forty-four, Jesus repeated His point of verse thirty-seven, but more emphatically. He explained "no one can come to Me, unless the Father who sent Me draws him," which means no one, either a Jew then or someone today, can come to Jesus of his own volition. In an argument similar to rabbinical teaching, Jesus explained this was impossible. No one came to Jesus unless the Father drew that person. The statement in verse forty-four is the opposite thought of verse thirty-seven, which explains how the Father gave to the Son, and that all whom the Father gave, Jesus would not cast out. In verse forty-four, Jesus noted that none could come to Him unless the Father drew that individual.

Jesus then repeated His message in a different way, combining verses from Isaiah 53:13 and Jeremiah 31:34, that God had taught His people and everyone who heard and learned from Him would come to Jesus. Jesus reiterated that no one had ever seen the Father except the One, who came from the Father, and no one could see Him because of His holiness except for Jesus, who came from the Father. It was Jesus who taught about the Father "for through Him we hear and learn from His Father. This completely explains how the Father draws to the Son, and how by His drawing He gives to the Son." [78]

Jesus concluded with, "I am the bread of life," which repeated His earlier statement. The idea of "eating" and "drinking" to denote accepting the truth and contemplating its implications was not unheard of for the Jews. Deuteronomy 8:3, Jeremiah 15:16, and Ezekiel 2:8-10 used the same symbolism or metaphor as Jesus. We use like metaphors of someone eating or swallowing. You hear of someone who "devours" a favorite book or a naïve individual who "swallows" a lie. We understand these expressions to be metaphors, and, in the same way, Jesus told the Jews they had to "eat" His flesh and "drink" His blood. This statement was metaphorical meaning they had to incorporate the Messiah into their innermost being and to intimately share His life.

Because of superficial similarities between the eating of bread and drinking of wine (even though there is no mention of wine in this passage) and the Lord's Supper, early church scholars suggest this passage refers to it in some way. However, an examination of the words seems to reject this idea, not to mention the fact that He did not institute this sacrament until the very end of His ministry and the underlying premise was paschal symbolism. Further, bread and wine commonly referred to a meal, since the two were basic components of the daily diet at the time of Jesus. Also, the word He spoke in this passage was "flesh," whereas in other places in the New Testament when He referred to the ceremonial eating of bread and drinking of wine, He said "body," which conveys a different meaning.

"Flesh" in this particular verse is reminiscent of John 1:14. The interpretation of flesh and blood to mean the Lord's Supper was popular with the early church, but by the Protestant Reformation, it had fallen out of favor. Even Catholics have deprecated their support of this interpretation. An indirect backwards reference to the Lord's Supper may exist as the essential premise of the celebration is the memory of the body and blood of Jesus, but we should see this as a coincidence.

A new thought begins in verse forty-nine and is an inclusio that continues through verse fifty-eight. We must read these verses as an entity, and the thoughts within in them interconnect and interrelate. Jesus returned to the original topic of the manna the Israelites received through Moses and explained that, even though they ate the manna, they nevertheless died. However, He was the bread that came from heaven, and if they ate, metaphorically, this bread, they would not die. He repeated that He was the living bread that came from heaven and whoever believed in Him had eternal life. The Jews again grumbled at His words only to hear Jesus repeat Himself. Once again, they heard His words on the plain or p'shat level rather than the spiritual or d'rash level. To metaphorically eat His flesh and drink His blood is necessary for eternal life. Those who refuse this command of Jesus have no life.

To counter this grumbling of the Jews, Jesus, for the fourth time, used the double amen "truly, truly" to emphasize He was speaking deliberately and purposefully. Those who seek eternal life and resurrection on the last day must eat His flesh and drink His blood. The thought in verse fifty-four is similar to that of verse forty. It is important to note the verse tense for these actions is aorist, meaning a one-time event, not a continual activity. This further discounts the idea that this passage refers to the Lord's Supper Communion. "Eating and drinking Christ's flesh and blood thus appears to be a very graphic way of saying that people must take Christ into their innermost being." [79] The way Jesus expressed the flesh and blood as separate entities also hinted forward to His crucifixion where flesh and blood were again separate. He again emphasized how His flesh was true food and His blood was true drink, speaking, of course, metaphorically. He told the crowd, again, that the Father had sent Him and reiterated His dependence on the Father.

The reference to manna is the closing of the inclusio that began in verse forty-nine. "The contrast is now made explicit. Manna is no food of eternal life; those who ate of it died. Those who eat the Bread which is Christ never die." [80] The opponents of Jesus referred to the manna that was given to the Israelites during their time in the wilderness and challenged Him to provide manna. Jesus replied, while the manna was vital for the physical survival of the Jews, it only dealt with the physical, not the spiritual. Those who ate the manna died like everyone else. However, they should consider the manna from a spiritual perspective, that the manna from heaven gave eternal life. The true manna that came from heaven, namely Jesus, was different, and anyone who ate this manna would not die, but have eternal life.

CHAPTER NINE

THE FOURTH SIGN
FEEDING THE FIVE THOUSAND

JOHN 6:1-15

The fourth sign, occurring during the Galilean ministry of Jesus, reveals His authority over quantity. This sign happened after He returned to Galilee from Judea, but the precise time is unclear. It is known to have been during the springtime in the weeks before the Jewish Passover, which in 32 CE would have been April 13 and 14. This chapter begins with "after these things," which is how the Apostle John typically indicates an indeterminate passage of time. In this case, he is referring to the approximate year of Jesus' Galilean ministry. He had returned to the area and made Capernaum the base of operations. Jesus then sent the disciples out preaching the kingdom of heaven.

The results were so spectacular that even Herod Antipas wondered if John the Baptist, whom he had beheaded, had come back to life. The evangelizing by the disciples probably took anywhere from two weeks to several months, during which time Jesus likely remained in Capernaum, which was a better location to base a ministry for many reasons. It was within walking distance of Perea and the border of Philip's rule, which would have been advantageous given the capriciousness of Herod Antipas; yet Capernaum would not have attracted unwanted attention from Roman authorities.

Upon completion of their preaching, the disciples returned to report the good news. Likely because of the increase of interest from Herod Antipas, Jesus traveled by boat to the eastern side of the Sea of Galilee, which was in the jurisdiction of Philip. The Sea of Galilee was known as Kinnereth in the Old Testament because the shape of the lake was of a lyre, and in New Testament times it was known as Lake Tiberius from the city Herod Antipas built on the western shore around 20 CE and named after Emperor Tiberius.

The fact that all four Gospels (Matthew 14:13-23, Mark 6:31-46, Luke 9:10-17) record this event is interesting. The sixth chapter of John is the only chapter the Apostle John devotes to the ministry in Galilee while the other three Gospels contain considerably more of this phase of His ministry. Instead of proving collaboration, the differences, and agreements among the Gospels validate the historical accuracy of the account, which is not to say the four are radically different from each other. Rather, they provide a complete picture of the event. "The intent of this picture of Jesus—one presented with so much emphasis in all four Gospels—was to make visible the great future inaugurated in Jesus' coming and work as that had been repeatedly prefigured in prophecy under the image of the host presiding over and providing an abundant meal." [81]

Mark provides supplemental information about the plans of Jesus and His disciples to spend time alone. Once on the other side of the lake, Jesus and His disciples walked east to the foothills of the mountains, known today as the Golan Heights. From this vantage point, they could clearly see the Sea of Galilee and the plains, a place of peace and quiet to which Jesus frequently retreated. He sought refuge in such places sometimes with and sometimes without His disciples. Mark notes the grass in the region was green, which places the time of year in March or April just before the Passover. John is the only one of the four who notes it is the time of the Passover. "This point is no accident. The Passover was the start of the nation's day of liberation and led in a real sense to their 'life' as a nation, including the provision of manna to sustain them through Moses' leadership." [82]

The multitude, always seeking to be with Jesus, noted the direction the boat traveled and discerned the destination. The people trekked northwest from the region of Cana and Capernaum around the northern edge of the Sea of Galilee and turned southeast to go down the eastern side of the lake to be with Jesus. Once they arrived, Jesus, ever gracious and considerate, spent the good part of the day teaching until late afternoon, when it became evident food would become a pressing concern. With many men working as day laborers paid at the end of each day, existence was often meager, and it was not unusual to not have enough to eat each day. The Workers in the Vineyard parable explains the financial environment at the time of Jesus.

The Gospel of John picks up the account with a large crowd of people coming toward Jesus. This account does not mention the surrounding components of the story—of Jesus going to a place with His disciples to be alone, the teaching and healing He performed, or even the time of day it was when the sign occurred. No, the focus of the Apostle John is Jesus, and the Gospel is purposed to direct attention to Him. John, the writer, with a seemingly ruthless editor's pen, removes anything not pointing to Jesus. The observation by John of Jesus sitting with His disciples is not incidental. He often chooses a setting such as this where He was able to sit and yet look at His listeners as He taught. To sit is also a sign of authority which both Jesus and the Jewish rabbis utilized. The history of the Jewish people is replete with religious experiences in the mountains including Abraham and Isaac, the Ten Commandments, and the location of Jerusalem, and the Temple, to name a few. At the time of Jesus, mountains were almost synonymous with religious experiences.

Having told the disciples of the need to feed the multitude, Jesus turned to Philip to seek his input as to the best solution to the situation. Being from Bethsaida, a nearby village (John 1:44) it would make sense he would know where they could acquire a significant amount of food on short notice. The manner in which the Fourth Gospel presents the interaction between Jesus and Philip reveals Jesus was testing him in spiritual matters. It is equally clear from the passage that Jesus already had a solution in mind.

The response of Philip, who is called by some a financial pessimist, focused on the limitation of human resources and abilities, ignoring the divine power available through Jesus. This perspective is evident as he lamented that even 200 denarii, nine months' wages for a day laborer, would not have been sufficient for all the people to enjoy even a small amount of food. He, like the other disciples, forgot the resources available through Jesus. The number two hundred to which Phillip referred is significant because it often designates insufficiency in Scripture.

Andrew, the brother of Simon Peter, demonstrated his willingness to help, coming to Jesus with the news of a little boy willing to contribute his meager amount of food. Even though the focus of Jesus seems to have been on the spiritual growth of Philip, Andrew revealed his spiritual maturity by bringing a possible solution to Jesus. The offering of barley bread or small cakes (hardly loaves) and two fish—thought by most commentators to be little, pickled or salted—was meant as an appetizer. It is debatable who took the initiative in offering the small amount of food to Jesus; could it have been that rather than Andrew finding even a meager supply of food and bringing the boy to Jesus, the boy came to the disciple and, not knowing what else to do, Andrew brought him to Jesus?

Barley bread was fare for the poor as those who could afford it ate bread made of wheat or another better grain. "Barley loaves appear explicitly in Elisha's miracle of feeding one hundred men in 2 Kings 4:42-44, a passage with sufficient parallels to the Gospel's feeding miracles to suggest deliberate allusion." [83] Andrew, recognizing the impending crisis and thinking to investigate the options to provide food or hearing the question asked of Philip, brought the little boy to Jesus. It is noteworthy that the second time the Gospel mentions Andrew, he is again bringing someone to Jesus. The first time is at the beginning of the Gospel when he brings Simon Peter, his brother, to Jesus. Outside of these two mentions, we find virtually nothing of this disciple, but the fact he is willing to bring the situation to Jesus speaks of his devotion.

Jesus instructed the people to sit down, which they did in groups of fifty and one hundred (Mark 6:40). According to the Gospel accounts, there were five thousand men. Jesus took the loaves of bread and fish, thanked the Father for the food, and began to break off pieces of fish and bread to distribute to the disciples who, in turn, passed the food to the crowds (Matthew 14:18, Mark 6:41, Luke 9:16). John's account focuses on the amount of food; everyone had as much as they wanted in contrast to Philips statement that, even if two hundred denarii were available, the multitude would have received only a meager portion. As a note, the number two hundred in this passage is a multiple of twenty, which is the number for vain expectancy or waiting in vain. There are several references to twenty in the Old Testament that indicate a hopeless waiting or a period less than the appointed time of deliverance.

When the multitude had eaten—probably somewhere around 12,000 to 15,000 persons since the tally in the Gospel was 5,000 men—Jesus commanded the people to collect the remaining bread. They then fill twelve baskets with the leftovers. There is an ongoing debate on the meaning of the number twelve, with some suggesting the number represented the twelve tribes of Israel and that Jesus was able to provide for all of God's people while other suggestions include the twelve disciples or some other symbolism.

While there is likely some significance, it was probably readily apparent to the first and possibly second generation of people who read the Fourth Gospel, but the actual meaning has most likely been lost to antiquity to us who read the Fourth Gospel today. Also, food and drink were seen at the time of Jesus to mean prosperity and right relation with God. It was also a metaphor for blessings. This concept, presented in both a negative and a positive manner, can be seen in numerous Old Testament verses.

There are many hints or references in the actions of Jesus to Moses and the Israelites during their time in the Wilderness. The sign presents Jesus as the fulfillment of a type of Moses. "Under Moses' leadership, Israel escapes through the Red Sea, travels through the wilderness and miraculously receives food there. These stories are now echoed in Jesus' miraculous feeding of the five thousand and his rescue of his disciples as he walks to them on the sea." [84] Jesus supplied the physical needs of the people in a way they could not understand, just as God had provided manna and water to the Israelites.

The setting in the wild, uninhabited country east of the Sea of Galilee is reminiscent of the Wilderness into which Moses led the Israelites. This motif continues later in the chapter when Jesus referred to Himself as the "living bread," which, again, was meant to remind His Jewish audience of how God provided for their forefathers. In this instance, just as in so many other encounters between Jesus and the Jewish crowds, they misunderstood Him. Alternatively, maybe not so much misunderstood, but the people only saw the action of Jesus on the simple or p'shat level and were unable to perceive the underlying messages or meanings, the remez and midrash levels of what Jesus was trying to communicate.

After the people collected the left-over bread and counted the baskets, they saw the symbolism of the twelve baskets. With the Passover approaching with its focus on the deliverance of God's people from slavery and the increase in nationalism, pilgrims who lived in the region who were planning to travel the distance to Jerusalem decided instead to see this fellow Jesus, who was performing miraculous signs. Passover was "when the Jewish people recalled their deliverance from Egypt through Moses and were looking for the Prophet like him who was to come." [85] People began to realize the sign to say Jesus was the Prophet, who was to come into the world, and the stirring of a notion to make Jesus their king (6:14-15) began to develop in the multitude.

It is noteworthy that all the Gospels note the number of men present. The men, 5000 in number, would have constituted a military force for anyone with the ambition to assume leadership, and verse fifteen indicates the men in the crowd were looking for such an individual. If they had imitated the tactics of the Maccabees several hundred years before, they would have been a difficult opponent for the Romans. With these thoughts in the minds of some of the men in the multitude, they sought to make Jesus their king and leader of the revolution. The multitude used Deuteronomy 18:15-19 as their justification.

If this man Jesus was indeed the Prophet, he would lead them from bondage and oppression just as Moses had in Egypt. The Passover festival contained two aspects: the passing over of the first born in Egypt in the tenth plague and the release from Egyptian captivity through the intervention of Yahweh. Passover was the picture of God miraculously stating His claim to the Israelites, releasing them from Egyptian captivity, rescuing them from imminent death through the waters, and providing food and water in the Wilderness.

For this reason, this sign was incredibly significant to the Jews who had come to Jesus. The attitude of the crowd, as John explains "reveals, more clearly perhaps than any other portion of Scripture, the kind of Messiah the people wanted; someone who would be able and willing to provide for their physical needs. When it seemed to them Jesus would actually fulfill this expectation, they were anxious to lead him in triumph to Jerusalem, if need be by force, in order to crown him king." [86]

Consequently, they wanted to anoint Jesus their leader or king to overthrow the Roman occupation and establish a kingdom in which all would have plenty to eat and drink and enjoy the blessings of God. John "does not suggest that the people were wrong in identifying Jesus as the coming prophet; he does suggest that they were wrong in interpreting his significance on a material and external plan." [87] Jesus, perceiving their intentions, withdrew from them by going up the mountain where He could be by Himself. "If Christ had allowed them to make Him king then, His spiritual kingdom would have been ruined, the Gospel would have been stamped with everlasting infamy, and the hope of salvation would have been completely destroyed." [88] Before leaving Jesus dismissed the crowd and told the disciples to get into the boat to return across the Sea of Galilee.

The dreams and aspirations of the multitude were on the physical plane while those of Jesus were on the spiritual. Thus, the two were incompatible. Jesus was cognizant of the motives of the crowd and instructed the disciples to return to Capernaum from Bethsaida. There was a significant potential because the disciples did not yet understand the spiritual aspect of the kingdom of heaven, they might have fallen under the influence of those who sought a restoration of the Davidic kingdom with Jesus as king. In all the Gospel accounts, Jesus clearly wanted to deal with the people apart from the disciples. The type of king to which the multitude was seeking to elevate Jesus was not the sort of kingship He sought. Thus, He dismissed the crowd and went up the mountain to pray where He could not be followed or found.

Since the time of Jesus, three views to this event have emerged. One is that, when Jesus began to distribute the bread and fish to the disciples to pass to others, others who were there with Jesus decided to share their food with those around them. The miracle, then, occurred in the hearts of those who were there with Jesus on the Golan Heights. The second view is that the food Jesus provided was a sacrament or ritualistic meal, with each receiving a minuscule portion, much like the Lord's Supper or Communion. These suggestions, even though they have their advocates, downplay the divinity of Jesus and offer only rationalistic explanations of the event.

Most scholars soundly reject these explanations, especially since they repudiate the accounts in the four Gospels. The third view is that the sign occurred just as in the four Gospel accounts: Jesus miraculously distributed the bread and fish until the entire throng was satisfied, and afterwards, the people had gathered twelve baskets. John stresses the fact that all the people had plenty to eat and were satisfied. The amount of food Jesus provided was vastly greater than the two denarii Philip had suggested would barely feed the multitude. This interpretation is the only realistic view to take of this sign and one which recognizes the happening as truly miraculous, revealing another aspect of the divinity and messianic claims of Jesus.

CHAPTER TEN

THE FIFTH TEACHING
THE LIFE-GIVING SPIRIT

JOHN 7:14-29

Jesus returned to Jerusalem for the Feast of Tabernacles after spending time ministering and teaching in Galilee. He revealed His presence during the feast and began teaching in one of the courts surrounding the Temple. Many who are there had never heard Him speak before, although they had heard of Him. As with His other teachings, the words of Jesus provoke controversy.

In the verses before His appearance in the Temple, there is no implication that Jesus sought to hide His activities or work in secret. However, because Galilee was far away from Jerusalem and separated by Samaria, things that happened there were "secret" as far as those who live in Jerusalem knew. If anyone wanted to make a messianic claim, it should have occurred in the holy city of Jerusalem before the religious leaders. Possibly for this reason or maybe less-than-friendly reasons, the brothers of Jesus urged Him to attend. However, to go to the feast when His brothers suggested would not have been the right time.

The beginning verses of this passage reveal that Jesus, seemingly contrary to what He had told His brothers, namely that His time was not right (John 7:6), did go to the Temple during the middle of the event. That Jesus attended the feast implied that the Father instructed Him to go even though He had told His brothers of His intentions to not participate. That Jesus went to Jerusalem did not make His earlier words to His brothers false or misleading, for, at the time, the will of the Father was for Jesus to remain in Galilee. This incident does, however, point out the increasing degree of isolation from others that Jesus was experiencing, even from His immediate family.

The Feast of Tabernacles lasted for eight days, and Jesus, showing no fear for His personal safety, boldly revealed Himself on day four or five. The appearance of Jesus at the Temple was the fulfillment of Zachariah chapter fourteen, which prophesies the sudden appearance of the Lord at His temple. A similar prophecy can be found in Malachi 3:1. The people were surprised for two reasons. First, His very presence at the

Temple signifies some degree of legitimacy. Second, the manner of His teaching was unlike how the rabbis taught. The Temple comprised the main building with several courts or porticos, such as the court of the women, the court of the men, and the court of the Gentiles, and Jesus likely taught at one of those locations, most likely the court of (Jewish) men. The wording in these verses suggests many in the crowd while they may have heard of Jesus, had never seen Him, which is consistent with the fact that John does not have any record in his Gospel of Jesus preaching or teaching previously in Jerusalem.

The people with whom Jesus interacted during the Feast of the Tabernacles were of one of three groups, and this division may have been exacerbated by the presence of Galilean Jews who supported Jesus. One of the groups comprised the Jews and religious leaders who sought to kill Him. They perceived Jesus as a threat to their place and stature. Most of the time when the Fourth Gospel mentions the Jews seeking Jesus, this mindset is the context. The second group defended Jesus, believing His character to be stellar and His contribution beneficial. The third group thought Him an imposter and a deceiver of the people.

By His very presence in the Temple and His preaching to the crowd, Jesus challenged the Jews who are at the Temple and put the "audience in a dilemma. Is He a true messenger from God to be heeded? Or is He a false prophet who should be executed?" [89] The teaching of

Jesus "produced critical amazement and bewilderment among those who heard Him in the temple, not astonishment over His knowledge, but offense. How could this man, who had never received the appropriate training act as one instructed in the Scripture?" [90] Another factor of His teaching, which was offensive to the Jews, was He spoke as one with authority, not citing rabbinical precedent. When rabbis taught, they would cite previous rabbinical authority for a position or opinion in a way similar to an attorney citing prior case law in a court proceeding.

In response, Jesus explained the origin of His message was divine, but the source of His training was not. Those listening questioned His qualifications, and He, in turn, questioned the focus or purpose of their attentiveness. Pink astutely writes that their reactions to Jesus truly revealed their hearts. "It was not their consciences that were exercised, but their curiosity that was aroused. It was not the claims of God they were occupied with, but the schools of men. It was not the discourse itself they were pondering, but the manner of its delivery that engaged their attention." [91] As Jesus Himself noted, no one comes to Him, unless the Father draws him; here in this passage is a perfect, yet tragic, illustration of a crowd not drawn by the Father to Jesus.

Jesus explained His message was divine. To support His claim, Jesus said, if anyone wanted to verify whether His teachings were true, he should do the will of God, and he would discover the teachings of Jesus came from

God and were true. If He had claimed to be self-taught or that no teacher was necessary for Him, the crowd would immediately and rightfully discredit and ignore Him. As Kostenberger dryly notes, the culture at the time of Jesus did not prize originality. To be seen offering radically new ideas was dangerous and possibly subversive. In the same way, people would perceive the practice of not citing rabbinical precedent as arrogance and a significant departure from time-tested and revered tradition.

Jesus explained the people could judge Him and see He was not seeking glory or honor for Himself. Because His single purpose was to bring glory to the Father, what He said was true, and they could trust Him because He was not seeking His glory or honor. In verse nineteen, Jesus then moved to the topic of the Law and how none of the Jews kept the Law. Not only were they not keeping the Law (and Jesus expressed this with a rabbinical expression which meant to act or behave in a manner to obey the law), they also could not perceive Jesus was perfect in His obedience to the Law.

Jesus explained how the "Law came through Moses, though its ultimate origin, like that of the manna, is from God Himself, and parts of it were given to the fathers before Moses. But the Law could be misinterpreted and abused to judge others inconsistently." [92] To demonstrate a case in point, Jesus cited the Law against murder (Exodus 20:13) and called for the religious leaders to be held accountable because they were seeking to kill Him. The crowd, mostly consisting of pilgrims from distance places, knew little of the conflict between Jesus and the local religious authorities, and assumed the claims of Jesus to be those of a delusional individual. They questioned His assertion of the murder plot and accused Him of having a demon, asking who wanted to kill Him.

Rather than focusing on the actions of His opposition, Jesus responded in verse twenty-one by referring to one miracle and how it was arousing such animosity toward Him. Given the location of this event, the miracle or sign to which Jesus referred was the healing of the man crippled thirty-eight years at the pools of Bethesda. This sign was the only one He performed in Jerusalem. In His argument with the Pharisees about the Sabbath, the point He tried to make was that His actions, in reality and spirit, fulfilled the original purpose of the Sabbath and the Pharisees should stop judging using an invalid measure. If they judged, they should apply the right standard. Jesus then presented an argument from the Old Testament to support why His healing of the ill man did not violate the Sabbath. Jesus referenced the practice of circumcision from Genesis 17:10, which was established by the patriarchs long before Moses.

When God gave the Mosaic Covenant to the Jews, there already existed a covenant between God and Abraham, the father of the Jews, known as the Abrahamic Covenant. The Mosaic Covenant, known as the Mosaic Law, was given to supplement the first covenant and did not invalidate the first, which included the practice of circumcision. The practice of circumcision continued and deemed permissible even on the Sabbath because of its inclusion in the Abrahamic Covenant, although technically it was work and violated the Sabbath rules in the Mosaic Law.

Jesus was not arguing against the Sabbath or opposing the laws prohibiting work on the Sabbath; He was seeking to fulfill the true meaning of Judaism. In the same way, the practice of circumcision was accepted on the Sabbath, should not the healing of a man's physical infirmities be accepted in the same manner? Jesus urged the crowd to judge not on appearance, but on what was right. There is an implication in this statement that the people were guilty of wrongly judging in this specific situation, and they needed to adjust or correct their perspective.

At this point, the conversation returned to the original question of who was this man, Jesus. The crowds began to question the presence of Jesus. The Apostle John differentiates between the crowds who supported Jesus and the religious leaders who, after initial general acceptance, adopted an aggressive and critical attitude toward Jesus. That Jesus was free to speak openly and was seemingly immune to arrest, much less be the target of any legal action, seems to have indicated to the crowds that the religious leaders, despite their heated rhetoric and sometimes not-so-veiled threats, were in the actual process of determining whether Jesus was the Messiah.

Verse twenty-seven notes the argument or discussion concerning the Messiah continued among the crowd and that they knew where Jesus came from, presumably Galilee, but that the origin of the Messiah was a mystery. This verse seems to indicate the crowd rejected His messianic claim in the course of the debate because they understood, based on rabbinical teaching, the Messiah would appear seemingly out of nowhere, and His origins would be unknown. In contrast to this rabbinical teaching, they "knew" Jesus came from Nazareth in Galilee, and that invalidated His messianic claim. Others in the crowd who were knowledgeable of Old Testament messianic prophecy knew the Scripture claimed the Messiah would not come from Nazareth but Bethlehem.

As far as they knew, Jesus hailed from Nazareth in, of all places, Galilee, which was the exact response of Nathanael when the new disciple Philip told him of the Messiah. As an aside, the magi and scribes presented Old Testament prophecies to Herod when they told him the Messiah was to be born in Bethlehem. Later in the same chapter, John notes some in the crowd also knew Bethlehem was the birthplace of the Messiah. Some may have had held different interpretations of the coming of the Messiah, and others simply may not have known the details of the messianic prophecies in the Old Testament.

At the end of this discourse, Jesus cried out, having divine knowledge of the thoughts of the crowd. For the Gospel narrative to note that He cried out suggests His statement was important. Jesus revealed to the crowd that He was not acting on His initiative, but the Father had sent Jesus, and He who had sent Jesus was true. Jesus knew the Father because He was from the Father and the Father had sent Him. If the crowd truly knew the Father, they would accept Jesus whom the Father had sent. If, however, they did not know the Father, how could they know the Son whom the Father sent?

CHAPTER ELEVEN

THE FIFTH SIGN
WALKING ON THE WATER

JOHN 6:16-21

The fifth sign happened closely after the feeding of the five thousand on the east side of the Sea of Galilee. "John does not call attention to this miracle, and it is possible that it is included mostly because it was attached historically to the previous miracle of the multiplication of the loaves." [93] This sign reveals the authority of Jesus over the laws of nature. After Jesus had dismissed the multitude, He went up the mountain to pray. He had told the disciples to wait for His arrival at Bethsaida and if He did not join them, to depart via boat for Capernaum on the other (north-west) side of the Sea of Galilee. Matthew and Mark confirm that Jesus instructed the disciples to depart for Capernaum.

These two Gospels provide additional details of the circumstances surrounding the fifth sign not found in the Fourth Gospel. The three accounts taken together provide a complete picture of the events on the Sea of Galilee. "In general, John's account is by far the shorter. It is told more from the viewpoint of the disciples who are waiting for Jesus while the Synoptic account is from the viewpoint of Jesus who is alone on the land and sees the disciples distressed" [94] in the storm.

Morris and other scholars believe Jesus gave instructions to the disciples to wait for Him at Bethsaida until a certain time and, if He had not joined them, to set off for Capernaum. This interpretation would explain the seeming inconsistency of the account in Mark with the other accounts. The narrative in the Fourth Gospel tells how the disciples went to the Sea of Galilee and that it was evening when they embarked on the small boat to Capernaum. Carson and Borchert both note the reference to darkness and the likelihood the words contain a double meaning as in similar mentions in the Fourth Gospel. The darkness of the night journey by the disciples and the absence of Jesus are strongly connected. The disciples obeyed the command of Jesus and traveled across the Sea of Galilee from the north-east corner of the body of water with their destination the north-west corner, which was not directly across from Bethsaida.

However, the boat did venture into the Sea of Galilee away from the shore. According to the timeline, they cast off in the early evening. Pliny, an ancient historian, writes that the Sea of Galilee was six miles wide and sixteen miles long. Josephus notes in his prolific writings the lake was one hundred furlongs long by forty furlongs wide. Since about eight furlongs make up a mile, these descriptions are consistent. Also, the Apostle John, as well as several of the other disciples, grew up on the Sea of Galilee and made their livelihood as fishermen. Of all the accounts of the seven signs in the Fourth Gospel, this was the one in which they were intimately aware of the setting.

Reading the passages telling of the experience, the disciples, having rowed all night, were suddenly faced with a storm that caused serious problems for the small craft. They faced a strong head wind and made little, if any, progress. The boat headed west with the disciples facing east, the direction from which they had come, as they rowed. Topographically, the Sea of Galilee was some six hundred feet below sea level and much lower than the surrounding region, and it would often cause problems for small crafts. The Sea of Galilee "was situated below sea level in a bowl in the hills, and the defiles between the hills acted as chimneys that directed the concentrated blasts of wind down upon the water.

Also, because of the relatively shallow depth of the lake, it was subject to violent storms that were the terror of the fisherman who ventured upon it." [95] Cool air would come from the south-east and cause severe turbulence when it came in contact with the warm, humid air near the Sea of Galilee. Squalls would often occur, and any boat on the water would be in danger of capsizing or being swamped. Storms in the Sea of Galilee are so dangerous that even modern boats with powerful engines do not venture far into the body of water; the effect of such storms on a small boat would be just that much more dangerous.

At this point in the narrative, John changes the tense to active voice to emphasize the drama but focuses more on the action of Jesus relieving the fears of the disciples over seeing what they believed was an apparition. In the midst of all this, in the middle of the night, likely exhausted by the excitement of the feeding of the five thousand and now in the midst of a storm, Matthew and Mark noted a figure, seemingly a ghost, walking toward them on the water. Quite naturally, they were terrified. Not that they were afraid because of the storm, because "some of them, at least, were used to the lake and its storms, and there is no indication that they were afraid before they saw Jesus." [96] Both Mark and John use language meaning that Jesus was "on" rather than "by" the Sea of Galilee.

The account that the disciples were terrified when they first saw Jesus does not correspond with the suggestion of being near the shore and spotting Him walking along the shore. Had they noticed Him walking along the shore, as some critics would have it, it would not have prompted such a reaction, "a fear that apparently also prevented the disciples from immediately recognizing Jesus in the approaching figure. For they had never learned to know Him in that way and thus, in that place and horrendous situation, had not expected Him at all." [97] The potent combination of exhaustion, the danger and stress of the storm, and the lateness of the hour weakened the spirits of the disciples, causing them to be susceptible to superstitions and folk stories.

As a note of explanation for those not familiar with the Passover, the celebration focused on more than just the lamb whose blood was shed to mark the doorposts of the Israelites to protect their first-born from the angel of death. It was a remembrance of the entire episode of the exodus from the escape from Egypt through the Red Sea to the eating of the manna that God provided in the Wilderness. This relationship and the emotional connection of Jesus providing bread to the multitude and walking on the water were natural to the Gospel writers Matthew and Mark. Readers of the Fourth Gospel from a Jewish perspective would recall Old Testament passages such as Job 9:8 and Psalm 77:16-20 of God being the One who walks on water.

Interestingly, Luke does not mention this event in his Gospel, but being a Gentile, was likely not aware of the Passover symbolism of the bread and the water. The Apostle John, on the other hand, does not mention the emotions of the disciples when they first see Jesus. He spares no words on the fears of the disciples, for his focus is on the alleviation of their fears, on Jesus speaking the words, "It is I." When the disciples recognized the figure, they took Him aboard. According to the Fourth Gospel, "all at once the boat, which when Jesus went aboard was still a long way from shore, was at the land where they were going," [98] which suggests the boat was moved instantaneously and miraculously from the middle of the lake to its destination. According to all three accounts, the boat was about three miles from the eastern shore of Bethsaida, which would have made them about two miles from their destination of Capernaum. Is it not possible that, when Jesus climbed aboard the boat, He performed another sign or miracle and immediately brought the vessel and its occupants to their destination?

Scholars have advocated this interpretation that the boat moved immediately to its destination, and a strict interpretation supports this idea. Certainly, Jesus had shown similar authority in the presence of the disciples. We know Jesus is the Lord of time and distance. This explanation provides the most reasonable explanation of the narrative in the Fourth Gospel and does not contradict or cause difficulty with the accounts in Matthew or Mark. As the miraculous transport of the boat to its destination does not add to the purpose of the Fourth Gospel, the author does not emphasize this deed by Jesus.

CHAPTER TWELVE

THE SIXTH TEACHING
THE CHILDREN OF ABRAHAM

JOHN 8:21-58

This passage, in many ways, is the apex of John's imagery associating Jesus with light and contrasting Him with the darkness. The passage contains supreme teaching by Jesus as well as the conflict between Him and the Jews. These verses also illustrate the confusion on the part of some in the crowd—whether genuine or contrived we cannot ascertain—and the way Jesus dealt with His detractors.

The occasion for this teaching occurred soon after the dramatic confrontation between Jesus and the accusers who caught a woman in the very act of adultery. Seeking to trap Him, they demanded the appropriate punishment for her transgression. Jesus stooped down, wrote in the dirt, looked up, and invited any who was without sin to cast the first stone, to which her accusers, beginning with the oldest, responded by departing. When Jesus was alone with the woman, He told her to also leave and to sin no more. Jesus and the Pharisees then had a heated discussion (8:12-20) concerning the validity of His Messianic standing and His witness of Himself.

In verse twenty-one, with little or no break in the action as the word “and” indicates, Jesus said, almost cryptically to the Pharisees, He was going away and they would seek Him but could not follow. This statement is similar to the one Jesus made in 7:33-34, but this time the words of Jesus were more ominous and understood to be referring to His death. The next statement of Jesus that He was from above and they from below was in line with the Judaic thought of God being in the heavenly realm above and man below in the created earth realm. This dichotomy of from above and from below can be seen throughout the ministry of Jesus. The Jews immediately understood Jesus. He was communicating two messages in His statements that He was departing and that they could not follow because they would die in their sins; His impending death and their sins would prevent them from being with Him. The expression “dying in sin” is from Proverbs 24:9, Ezekiel 3:18 and 18:18.

Jesus did not explain why they would want to follow but only that they would be unable to do so. "The incarnate Word is to be on earth in a visible form for a limited time only. This period is their opportunity: if they accept Him for what He is, then they will receive the right to become God's children; eternal life will be theirs." [99] Perhaps they would never repent; perhaps they would realize after His death the mistake made, or perhaps they would not be able to find His physical presence after His ascension. All of these are possible, but He did not explain here why they would not be able to follow Him.

The Jews reacted in confusion since they did not know what Jesus meant. They "persist in their trick of catching at some one word or expression in the utterances of Jesus, turning their venom on that, and blindly ignoring the grave substance of what Jesus says. So here they are deaf to the warning that they shall die in their sins, with all the horror that lies in this statement; they pick up only the expression that Jesus Himself is about to go away." [100] They speculated He might kill Himself, but quickly dismissed this notion. To the Jew, suicide was a significant sin and disqualified one from the future age. Jesus had made a similar statement earlier (7:33-34), and the crowd thought He meant He was going to Jews or Greeks outside the Promised Land, but this time they sensed, correctly, Jesus was referring to His own death.

The Jews were of earth and the seed of Adam, thus sinful. Also, they were not seeking the will of the Father or Moses. The two were of different realms that could not be made compatible. "He is a being of a different order, and thus, their pursuit of him when he chooses to leave them will be futile. It is because of this essential nature of theirs that he has told them that they will die in their sins. They belong to the world, the world where Satan is supreme. Therefore, when they die, they will die in their sins." [101]

The dialog continued between the crowd and Jesus with the crowd asking Jesus who He was. This conversation led to a discussion about Jesus and His relationship with the Father. "Their question shows how far they were from understanding what was most essential in Jesus' public ministry and how absurd it seemed to them that He held out faith in Him as the only way in which they could be saved." [102]

To answer the question, Jesus replied He had been telling them whom He was from the beginning, implying they did not want to accept His answer. He told the crowd He had many things to say about them, not to them. Because of the differences between Him and the listeners, the things He would say would be judgment. However, it was not the time then to judge, but He noted the words He spoke were true because of His relationship with the Father. The Apostle John notes in verse twenty-seven that the crowd did not understand the meaning in the words of Jesus and that He was talking about the Father.

Jesus continued speaking to the crowd in verses twenty-eight through thirty and told of His impending crucifixion. He explained that, when they lifted Him up, they would realize His true identity, implying He had been right from the beginning, and they had been wrong from the beginning. The relationship during this confrontation was irrevocably damaged because the Jews refused to accept His words, His claims, and His signs, and now Jesus had begun to reveal to them the future and all of its implications. His future death by crucifixion, a particularly gruesome way to die, was becoming clear, but Jesus was firmly resolute the Father who had sent Him had not abandoned, nor would abandon Him. "To the question 'Who are you?' no adequate answer will be given until the Son of Man has been 'lifted up'; that will be the definitive answer. The cross is the complete revelation of the divine glory manifested in the Son." [103]

It would also become apparent that His relationship with the Father He told them about was, in fact, the truth. His enemies would also come to realize He did nothing on His initiative, but did and spoke what the Father told Him to do and say. Jesus repeated that the One who sent Him, meaning the Father, was with Him because He was in the Father's will and always did the will of the Father and pleased the Father.

"There is a curious similarity between this passage and the discourse with Nicodemus. Both interpret belief and unbelief as light and darkness, respectively, and both present the cross or the 'lifting up' of the Son of Man as the point of separation between the two." [104] In both instances, it was not until His crucifixion that His true identity became known. The passage notes that many came to believe in Him, but many scholars believe this was a superficial belief and based on an error as the continuing passage indicates.

Jesus then spoke to those Jews who "believed" Him, and He explained that to believe in Him was to abide in His words and be truly free. This passage is one of the few times that we find the word "free" in all of the New Testament, and we should understand the meaning as freedom from the bondage of sin and moral darkness. This "is not talking about the eros of the human search for truth and the freedom this brings, on however high an intellectual or moral plane this may lie, but about the divine gift of freedom that liberates man from the deepest slavery of his human existence and gives him a share in the freedom of the Divine Spirit, in the glory of the divine life." [105]

Jesus had to speak firmly to those who claimed to believe, for they truly did not believe in their hearts but apparently accepted the logic and presentation of His arguments. The fact that the Apostle John refers to these new "believers" as "Jews" should reveal their true position. Jesus spoke the word "truth" seven times:

twice in verse thirty-two, and in forty, forty-four, forty-five, and forty-six. Truth in the Fourth Gospel is Jesus the Messiah as He is the true salvation and truth of the Father.

The crowd vehemently objected to what Jesus said claiming to be free because of their position as the offspring of Abraham and that they had never been slaves. This passage marks the first of eleven times the Fourth Gospel mentions Abraham, all of them in the last part of chapter eight, for it was through their relationship to Abraham the Jews assumed their freedom. As Kruse wrote, "this led to presumption. They believed that because they were Abraham's descendants, they would automatically inherit the kingdom of God. John the Baptist warned them not to presume upon this. Jesus warned that not all Jews would inherit the kingdom." [106]

Brown similarly notes that over the generations, "the sense of responsibility that accompanied the status of being a son of Abraham inevitably lost its sharpness, and for some, it was replaced by a sense of automatic divine protection." [107] For Jesus to imply they were, in fact, not free, denigrated a fundamental component of their hope, so the reaction, of course, was swift and forceful.

It should be evident that the crowd was claiming they had never been slaves in a spiritual sense because of their being descendants of Abraham. To claim to have never been enslaved politically or militarily is laughable because the Promised Land, thanks to its strategic location between the east and west, had been occupied by various foreign powers for hundreds of years and was even then subjected to Roman occupation. However, even though foreign powers were in control of the Promised Land, it was "true that even in servitude they maintained an independence of spirit which meant that they might be slaves in the body, but never in the soul." [108] This attitude was similar to the teaching of Jesus in which He noted the healthy do need a physician, but He had come to heal the ill and infirm who knew they were in need of attention.

Because of the intransigence of His critics and their refusal to realize their bondage to sin (verses thirty-four through thirty-eight), Jesus tried to clearly explain the differences between freedom and slavery and how allegiance to Abraham was a false hope. Jesus began with the double amen, or "truly, truly," to explain how anyone who continued in sin was a slave of sin. He also explained how the slave was not part of the house, making the slave-master relationship analogous to the relationship between a sinner and God.

The slave was unable to free himself, just as the sinner was unable to free self from sin, but Jesus could free the sinner from sin. The Jews based their hope on being the children of Abraham; theirs was the kingdom of heaven. Jesus explained that was not correct; their only hope for the future was to believe in Him. Jesus explained that the Jews, because of their sin, were descendants of a different father. They had not yet realized Jesus had just told them their father was not God or Abraham, but Satan; but this realization would be quick and the reaction furious.

The Jews, realizing Jesus was judging them, denied His words and repeated their claim of being descendants of Abraham. Jesus asked why they were trying to kill Him. Jesus had heard the truth from the Father, which Abraham could not have claimed; so if Abraham were truly their father, they would love Jesus because He came from the Father, the same God Abraham loved and obeyed. Jesus claimed that God was His Father, but, further, He implied His pre-existence in that He had come from God.

Jesus asked why they were not listening, and answered His question: it was because they could not hear His word. They responded by questioning His birth and father's identity, implying He was born out of wedlock or as the result of fornication. These verses suggest the Jews suffered a fatal flaw preventing them from coming to Jesus; they were so focused on their views, they were unable to perceive the words of Jesus because His words so offended them, thus proving what Jesus said was, in fact, true.

If God were truly the spiritual father of those Jews who opposed Jesus, they would have loved Him and accepted His messianic claims. Since they did not, this meant their spiritual father had to be someone other than God. Jesus began to reveal their true spiritual paternity and allegiance. He explained His opponents had a relationship with Satan and believed his lies. This explanation was an obvious hint or remez to the Genesis account of creation and its description of Satan. Since they were children of Satan, it was impossible for them to accept and believe in Jesus. They voluntarily did the will of Satan and the word Jesus spoke meant continual action and attitude—they were doing and were continuing to do Satan's will.

Verse forty-five is most insightful in that because Jesus spoke the truth, they did not believe Him because they could only hear the lie of Satan. Jesus challenged the Jews to convict Him of sin like His response when the Pharisees brought the woman caught in the act of adultery (John 8:3-11) to Him. The conversation continued and ultimately ended in a definitive statement by Jesus in which He proclaimed His deity. The Jews then insulted Jesus by claiming He was a Samaritan and was demon possessed in verses forty-eight and forty-nine. Jesus denied He had a demon, affirmed that He honored the Father, and said the Jews dishonored Him and, by extension, the Father.

Jesus explained He was not seeking His glory, but that there was One who judges. Those who believed and kept His word would not seek death, meaning spiritual death. There is a shift in verb tense to the present voice to indicate judgment was occurring then, not later. The

Jews denied Jesus, and their judgment was complete. The Jews, not understanding Jesus was speaking d'rash or spiritual rather than p'shat or plain level, replied that His statement only confirmed He had a demon. Their reasoning was that because everyone dies—Abraham, the prophets, and everyone else—yet Jesus was claiming that if anyone kept His word, they would not die. They asked Him whom He thought He was, which is similar to the question the Samaritan woman asked Jesus the same question.

Jesus briefly dropped the argument based on Abraham to tell the Jews that if He glorified Himself, He would be nothing. The Father glorified Him, but the Jews were seeking to disown Him. The Jews did not know the Father, but Jesus did. He knew the Father and kept His word and commandments. Starting at verse fifty-eight, Jesus returned to the argument about Abraham, upon which the Jews had placed their hope and security. Significantly, Jesus referred to Abraham as "your" father, rather than "our" father, which would have included Himself. Jesus explained that, unlike the Jews who opposed Him, Abraham rejoiced in Jesus. The Jews replied that Jesus was a young man and questioned how He could have seen Abraham. Jesus explained his eternity and deity and replied that before Abraham was, "I Am," at which point the Jews had heard enough and picked up stones to stone Him, but He hid and left the Temple.

CHAPTER THIRTEEN

THE SIXTH SIGN
HEALING THE MAN BORN BLIND

JOHN 9:1-41

The healing of the man born blind is, to this point, the most powerful sign demonstrating the Messianic claim of Jesus and His authority over misfortune. This healing also dramatically escalated the conflict between Jesus and the religious leaders. Because this healing was so spectacular and contained such a powerful messianic message, Chapter nine is devoted to this event and its repercussions. Also, the interaction between the formerly blind man and the Pharisees provides invaluable insight into the power of Jesus and the intransigence of the religious leaders.

This sign shatters misconceptions about the cause and purpose of calamity and reveals its relationship with sin. Of all the signs in this Gospel, the account and conversations concerning this event may be the most relevant today about sin and its impact. This healing was a powerful revelation and provided vivid credibility to the claims of Jesus, but also hardened the resolve of His enemies. This sign was not the only time Jesus healed a blind man (Matthew 9:27-31, Mark 8:22-26), but it was the only time He healed a person blind from birth. Not only did Jesus present His messianic claims through this healing, but it also occurred on the Sabbath.

Chapter nine is a continuation of Chapter eight, with no break in the action. The chapter opens with Jesus and His disciples presumably exiting the Temple, where He encountered the man blind from birth. The area surrounding the Temple was where beggars would gather seeking alms. For a blind person, begging was one of the few means of income. Jesus initiated the encounter when He noticed the blind man, possibly because of his calling for alms. From the wording of the passage, the disciples were familiar with the blind man, as were the locals. The disciples wondered what grave sin the man committed before birth or what sin the parents had committed to prompt such calamitous punishment, and they asked Jesus to reveal the reason for the man's condition.

The disciples seemingly assumed the role of a judge rather than seeking to provide alms from their funds or asking if Jesus could heal the man. Like today when we encounter a child with a congenital birth defect or some situation seemingly beyond human culpability, the disciples were puzzled by this man's malady and were unable to attribute it to a satisfactory reason. The unsurprising conclusion by the disciples, supported by verses such as Exodus 20:5, Exodus 34:7 and Numbers 14:18, was that his parents had grievously sinned. "Blindness was often associated with sin; in many cultures, it is natural to associate another's affliction with a specific avoidable cause to prevent anxiety on the part of those who speculated about the causes." [109] The disciples thought, as we sometimes do today, which an obvious cause and effect were necessary between sin and its consequences.

Jewish teaching explained such calamities as birth defects as being the result of sin. Some taught that a person could commit a sin before birth, citing Esau and Jacob. The pre-existence of the soul was another idea the rabbis used to explain congenital defects. According to these rabbis, all souls existed before the creation—in a seventh heaven or special place—awaiting a physical body in which to dwell. Before entering a body, the soul was already good or evil, with God administering punishment or reward to the soul's physical body at birth. A similar idea was reincarnation, which the Jews had acquired during the Babylonians exile.

According to this belief, the souls of men return over and over to earth, and any good or evil the person did carry forward to the next life as blessings or punishment. If a man, in a previous life, had been guilty of a heinous crime, when he returned he would suffer and experience poverty as punishment. While rabbinical teachings rejected this concept, this idea can be seen in the words of the disciples when Jesus asked them whom the people thought He was, and their answer ranged from John the Baptist to the Old Testament prophet Elijah and other well-known individuals.

Before addressing the blind man, Jesus made a general statement concerning the importance of carrying out the works of God while it was still possible. As long as it was the day, according to Jesus, the work of God would be done. There was considerable significance in Jesus doing the works of God so people would believe His messianic claims, and the opportunity for such work was drawing to a close because the night was coming. When Jesus healed the man's blindness, He allowed light to enter the man's world. As the light of the world, Jesus was working and revealing Himself as the Messiah, but the time was short, and He had to work quickly.

The words of Jesus being the light of the world are reminiscent of His "I Am" statement in 8:12, of which this sign was a continuation. While He was in the world, it was light because He was the light, but the impending crucifixion and burial meant darkness was approaching.

Throughout this entire chapter, there is a sense of foreboding or awareness that the time of light was drawing to a close. The darkness was the deepest during the three days between His crucifixion and resurrection. After He had arisen, the darkness began to recede as He revealed Himself to the disciples; it continued to recede as the Holy Spirit came to the disciples at Pentecost.

Jesus then specifically addressed the cause of the man's blindness. While He did not absolve the blind man or his parents from all blame or responsibility, He revealed that sin was not the fundamental cause of the blindness, contradicting Jewish theological thought at the time. We find a similar situation in the book of Job, which describes the numerous conversations between Job, his wife, and friends about the tragic events that suddenly befell Job. The problem was they lacked all of the pertinent information and, because of this lack of knowledge, were all incorrect. In the same way, the questions of the disciples were erroneous because they also made incorrect assumptions. The disciples had not advanced much further than the friends of Job about the true cause of pain and suffering.

Jesus explained that the man was blind so that the work of God might be manifested in him. The Old Testament basis for this statement could be the manner in which Yahweh dealt with Pharaoh in Exodus 9:16. We can discern this attitude in Luke 13:1-5 when Jesus explains the disasters were not because of the perceived greater degree of sinfulness of the victims. Calvin notes that sometimes it is not the intent of God to punish when He allows an affliction to impact a person's life, sometimes with significant consequences. The passage is not claiming that God caused the blindness to substantiate the Messianic claims of Jesus, but that Jesus overruled the condition of the fallen world to reveal the power of God.

This interpretation agrees with the situation of the man infirm for thirty-eight years. It was not the man's sin that had caused his condition, but the sin the man was committing brought the warning from Jesus that something worse would befall him if he did not repent. Jesus noted the man's calamity was intended to reveal the glory of God manifested through Him. It was the highest degree of exclusivity Jesus claimed for Himself; no other person was able to reveal the works of God.

After talking with the disciples, Jesus turned to the blind beggar. While the exchange with the disciples was insightful, the sign was not to determine the cause of the man's blindness but to demonstrate His messianic claim. According to the passage, Jesus spat on the ground and made clay with the spittle and dirt. He applied the mixture to the eyes of the blind man. "Like people in other cultures, Palestinian Jews apparently believed human excreta (including saliva) were forms of dirt rendering a person ceremonially unclean. Under certain conditions, however, it was believed that very 'dirt' could become an instrument of blessing in the hands of authorized individuals." [110]

Because of this general view of spittle, most rabbis frowned upon spittle as a curative entity. It is doubtful, given the context at the time, whether Jesus meant those around to perceive His spittle as magical; it was simply to form clay from the dirt to apply to the man's eyes and have it remain until he washed it off. The passage details this aspect of the healing because this was one of the points of which He was accused of violating the Sabbath.

Jesus communicated with the man through two of the primary senses of communication – hearing and touching. He instructed the man to wash his eyes at the pool of Siloam, the name of which means "sent." As Lenski and others note, it was no accident or chance Jesus instructed the man to wash in that specific pool. "Too often he (Jesus) speaks of his Sender and thus designates himself as the One Sent. He never acts without the most comprehensive insight." [111]

The pool in which Jesus instructed the man to wash was located in the extreme southern part of Jerusalem while the Temple was on the northern edge of the capital city. The pool of Siloam, which was large enough for a person to swim, was south-west of Mount Ophel, which meant the city of David, near the Tyropoeon Valley and the Valley of Hinnom. The source of water for the pool of Siloam was through Hezekiah's tunnel from the

Gihon spring. Hezekiah was the one who realized the danger the invader Sennacherib posed by possibly cutting the water supply to the city. He commanded engineers to make a passageway through solid rock for a water conduit from Gihon spring to Jerusalem. The conduit was approximately five hundred and eighty-five feet in length, and construction began at both ends and met in the middle, which was a remarkable achievement for the time. Archeologists discovered a tablet in 1880 commemorating the completion of the tunnel. Water sent through this tunnel was the reason for the name Siloam or "sent." Also, "it was the water from this same pool of Siloam used in the ceremony of the Tabernacles, and Jesus had said by way of replacement in 7:37-38, that He was now the source of life-giving water." [112]

As a point of validation, the Copper Scroll of Qumran also mentions the bathing basin at Siloam. This also meant the man had to travel a greater distance than permissible by Sabbath law. In giving this command, Jesus was increasing the man's faith through obedience. Neither the mud nor the water at the pool of Siloam had any more to do with the healing than the Jordan river where Elisha instructed Naaman to immerse himself seven times to be healed of leprosy (2 Kings 5:10, 13-14). In both cases, the fundamental concept is obedience.

Carson notes while John gives little attention to the spittle of Jesus beyond the necessary inclusion in the narrative, he is emphatic in explaining how the name of the pool, Siloam, meant "sent." Just as the Father sent Jesus into the world, so was the water sent to this pool, and so was the blind man sent to this specific pool to wash his eyes. Bultmann comments on the explanation of the meaning of the word Siloam, noting "the interpretation of the name, which has been added by the Evangelist if not indeed the editor, raises the symbolism of the narrative to the level of allegory." [113] As with other signs, Bultmann denies the miracle and seeks to relegate it to myth or existential explanation by the Gospel writers as their attempts to describe Jesus and in his analysis seems to deny the divinity of Jesus.

The in-depth account of the happening in the Fourth Gospel covers several aspects of the event and provides great insight into the world at the time of Jesus. The people, "who can find no explanation for the healing, bring the man to the Pharisees, whose judgment they are accustomed to respect. The Pharisees, who are on good terms with the people, are regarded as the people who are familiar with the Torah and its interpretation and the ones who must decide on matters of religious uncertainty." [114] The Pharisees summoned the man to investigate the event and the circumstances of the healing.

The implications of this sign were not lost on the religious leaders. Nowhere in the Old Testament is there recorded a blind person receiving sight, and there is also no account of anyone healing the blind in the New Testament outside of the actions of Jesus. To restore sight was viewed as a Messianic claim as stated in Isaiah 29:18, 35:5 and 42:6-7. While the intent of those who reported the healing to the Pharisees was not likely from spite, the Pharisees, nevertheless, convened a formal hearing. The charge "against Jesus would rest was plain: the healing involved a manifold breach of the Sabbath Law. The first of these was that He had made clay.

Next, it would be a question whether to apply any remedy on a holy day. Such could only happen in diseases of the internal organs, except when there was a threat to life or the loss of an organ. It was, indeed, declared lawful to apply, for example, wine to the outside of the eyelid, on the basis the act was washing; but it was sinful to apply it to the inside of the eye. "And as it regards saliva, its application to the eye is expressly forbidden, on the ground that it was evidently intended as a remedy." [115]

If this were not sufficient ground for an accusation, making and kneading the spittle and dirt constituted work. This legal hearing likely took place in the days following the Sabbath so the requisite participants could gather. At the time of the event, while the Pharisees were active in Jewish life, the Scribes were the experts in the Law and the Old Testament. To avoid confusion, the Apostle John refers to the opponents of

Jesus as Pharisees and later as Jews, referring to the religious leaders.

The interaction between the formerly blind man and the Pharisees contained several parts. The first was factual in nature in which the Pharisees determined, yes, the man was blind and, yes, he could now see. The Pharisees also investigated possible collusion between the man and Jesus. Through careful and probing questions, they sought deception by which to discredit Jesus. When talking to the Pharisees, the man was more cautious with his words; earlier when the people asked he explained how Jesus had made clay and anointed his eyes; when answering the Pharisees, he said Jesus applied clay to his eyes, not mentioning the making of the clay.

This action is possibly inconsequential but still interesting in that the formerly blind man did not mention Jesus kneading spittle and dirt into a paste before applying it to his eyes. He also did not say Jesus sent him to the pool at Siloam but only that he washed and could see. During the questioning, a division developed among the Pharisees because of the different training from the two major Pharisaic schools of the day. Pharisees of the Shammai School advocated that a man who heals on the Sabbath was a sinner. Those Pharisees of the Hillel school argued that a man who was able to perform good works was not a sinner. If a man were to violate the Sabbath law, he could not be of God because of the Sabbath violation. However, the fact He was able to heal the blind man surely revealed Jesus as being of God. The healing of the blind man by Jesus on the Sabbath exposed the differences between the Pharisees from these two schools and paralyzed the proceedings.

This event naturally led to the question as to how this Jesus acquired the power to heal. The Pharisees knew false prophets could produce false miracles as described in Deuteronomy 13:1-5. If Jesus did heal this man, how could He be a sinner, and if He were not a sinner, then what did His actions mean for Sabbath rules and prohibitions? It would be erroneous to simply assume the healing meant Jesus was from God; He was obviously a sinner because He violated the Sabbath. Furthermore, just as Moses was able to change his rod into a snake, so could the magicians of Egypt. Their confusion was evident by their questioning the man concerning the identity of his benefactor. In a normal meeting of this nature, the Pharisees would never have asked such a question, especially to someone unlearned as this man was, but ask they did.

The response of the man was unambiguous— "He is a prophet"—which only further infuriated the Pharisees and deepened their dilemma. The assessment by the formerly blind man revealed that he possessed considerable knowledge of the Old Testament. It was standard practice to evaluate a prophet on the signs he could produce. We can see this in the lives of Moses, Elijah, and other Old Testament prophets. The man healed was already beginning to perceive the situation with spiritual eyes that were gaining more and more insight while the Pharisees were descending into ever-deepening darkness. "They cannot believe that a Sabbath-breaker can be from God. The man cannot believe that one who had brought such great good into his life is not from God." [116] Interestingly, the Samaritan woman spoke a similar statement at Sychar's well, so it is interesting how the societal outcasts were able to discern the identity of Jesus while the religious authorities could not reach the same conclusion.

Not knowing the man and his formerly-blind state, the inquisitors sought to verify the legitimacy of the situation. It is worth noting in this portion of the passage John ceases to call them Pharisees and refers to them as Jews. This statement implies more intense animosity, and possibly higher-ranking religious authorities were now participating in the discussion. The topic turned to whether the man was truly blind from birth. The religious leaders summoned the two people who would surely know the facts: the parents. When asked to confirm their son's statement of his blindness, the parents affirmed he was their son, and he had been born blind, but they denied any knowledge and deferred the question to their son since he was of legal age to testify, being over the age of thirteen. The parents clearly saw the danger and had no desire to offend the powerful Pharisees and risk expulsion from the synagogue.

The comment and fears of the parents are interesting. Some have suggested John wrote this Gospel toward the end of the first century because of the threat of excommunication. However, even during the earthly ministry of Jesus, He spoke of men hating and excluding believers in the Beatitudes, but it is unclear whether the Jews had reached the point of excluding Christians from the synagogue. What may have been the case is that in Jerusalem the Pharisees would use honor and shame along with peer pressure to force believers out of the synagogue. Societal rules at the time of Jesus meant these tactics were likely effective, as people were fearful of expressing public support for Jesus. Because the religious leaders had decided to kill Jesus because of His threat to their position, it would make sense those in the synagogue who believed in Jesus would also have faced retribution.

Excommunication of different severities was used to remove from the synagogue: a short banishment to reprimand and a permanent ban called "cherum" or "herem" in Hebrew and 'anathema' in Greek. In this excommunication, the individual was cursed and banished from all ties with the Jewish community including family, vocation, and support. The person would be treated as a tax collector and sinner. To someone in the social-economic environment at the time of Jesus, such an event would have been traumatic and life-changing. There is insufficient information to determine the correct meaning of what John means by being put out of the synagogue.

With the parents unable to say what the Jews sought to hear, the Pharisees were on the horns of a dilemma. With no viable course of action, they turned their attention back to the formerly blind man and questioned him about what had happened. They also told the man to give glory to God, which was a command to confess the truth and expose Jesus as less than what He claimed. This exhortation is similar to the incident in Joshua 7:19-21 where Achan was confronted over his sin bringing judgment to Israel. The Jews may have also been seeking to show it was God who healed the man; all Jesus had done was apply some clay to the man's eyes and instruct him to go and wash them.

Therefore, it was not Jesus who brought sight to the man, but God. As Keener points out, the passage reveals how the agenda of the Pharisees to entrap Jesus warped their desire for truth. The statement by the Pharisees that "we know this man is a sinner" was the height of arrogance and a claim to absolute knowledge, which only the Father can claim. This incident is one of the most dramatic confrontations in all of the Scripture and reveals much of the mentality of the Pharisees and the dogged persistence and rich sarcasm of the formerly blind man.

Even though the man could not see, it is evident he possessed a quick wit and intelligence and was unafraid—perhaps to the point of foolhardiness—of the Pharisees. Instead of cowering to enable the Pharisees to control the direction of the Inquisition, the man asserted himself in dramatic fashion and put the Pharisees on the defense, a position from which they were never able to recover. The man recognized the attempts to verbally trip him or intimidate him into speaking what they sought to hear.

It was also obvious to all at the hearing that the Pharisees had lost all sense of objectivity in their quest to find fault with Jesus. This was likely why he "innocently" asked the Pharisees if they were asking him to tell them again of the event because they sought to become disciples of Jesus, which, of course, received an outraged response. Despite the pressure and arguments of the Pharisees, they could not persuade him from his position of being blind and now able to see. This single fact was enough, and all of the arguments raised up against it were futile.

The Jews then abandoned their arguments and tried to trump the debate by claiming to be disciples of Moses and questioning from where this man Jesus came. In many ways, this comprises the argument about Jesus in a nutshell. The Pharisees and religious leaders knew Moses and his teachings, but this Jesus was an unknown coming from, of all places, Galilee and offering a new revelation from God. The claim to being disciples of Moses was meant to point out the inferiority of being a disciple of Jesus.

Instead of being intimidated by this new argument, the man masterfully used irony to challenge their position, citing his healing and finding it remarkable they did not know from where Jesus came. He applied impeccable logic: if Jesus were not from God, then He could not have healed his blindness because God does not hear the call of the sinner, and Jesus could have done nothing apart from God. In making this argument, he echoed the teaching of the Hillel Pharisaic school. Needless to say, this argument threw them into another uproar.

The argument of the formerly blind man was impeccable and based on Old Testament teachings such as Psalm 34:15-17, Proverbs 15:29 and Ezekiel 8:18 for which they had no answer. Faced with utter defeat and having no tactical room in which to present any arguments, the Pharisees insulted the man and called him an apostate. They accused him of being born in sin, which, according to Jewish doctrine of the time, implied their agreement with his testimony of being born blind. "To their mind, he could not be Christ's disciple without defecting from the Law of Moses." [117] After their insults, the Pharisees banished him. "The context suggests that they not only pushed him out of the place where the interrogation was held but expelled him from synagogue membership, as his parents had feared might be done to them." [118]

Sometime later, Jesus found the man and invited him to become a follower. Jesus asked whether the man believed in "the Son of Man," which was one of His favorite self-expressions. Even though the man likely recognized the voice speaking to him, he asks the identity of the individual. Jesus revealed it was He who was the Son of Man. The man worshiped and professed faith. In the passage, John has Jesus in an immediate confrontation with the Pharisees, but this scenario is unlikely. What probably happened was that Jesus sought the man, revealed His identity, and accepted His worship.

Later, Jesus confronted the Pharisees. In this encounter, Jesus spoke cryptically to the Pharisees. He came into the world so those who could not see or recognize Him would be able to see or recognize Him and those who refused to see or recognize Him would become blind spiritually. This statement contains a hint or remez to Isaiah 6:9-10, and the Pharisees, surely recognizing the reference to Isaiah, asked Jesus if they were blind also. The response by the Pharisees reveals the depths of their spiritual condition and inability to see Jesus as the Messiah, despite His demonstration of opening the eyes of a man born blind. The comment by Jesus of their sins remaining implied no recourse or forgiveness for their guilt. This event was "more than a mere miracle, this sign represents a highly symbolic display of Jesus' ability to cure spiritual blindness. As the present story makes clear, the only sin against which there is no remedy is spiritual pride that claims to see while being, in fact, blind." [119]

CHAPTER FOURTEEN

THE SEVENTH TEACHING
THE GOOD SHEPHERD

JOHN 10:1-18

This teaching is a continuation of the previous chapter in which He had healed a man who had been blind from birth. This teaching occurred at the Feast of Dedication, also known as Hanukkah. In this passage, Jesus used several figures of speech and likened Himself to a shepherd, a figure to which almost everyone could relate either directly or through a family member or friend. As He had done before, Jesus took the familiar to convey a powerful lesson that reverberates even today with power and compassion.

This well-known and loved passage contains some new ideas and reveals more of the role of Jesus in salvation and the life of the believer. "Rightly understood, it is not only the last and highest announcement, but it contains and implies everything else. If the work of Christ is really that of the Father, and His working also that of the Father, then it follows that He 'and the Father is One.'" [120] As with most of His other teachings, the context through which to examine this passage is the Old Testament.

However, some of His words against thieves and robbers must also be understood to refer to His contemporaries, specifically the Pharisees and religious leaders of the day, in addition to those responsible for Judaism in the past. The shepherd's responsibility for the flock can be seen many times in the Old Testament, and the vocation of the shepherd was common at the time of Jesus. The Old Testament contains several passages condemning those shepherds who failed to guard their flock.

God the Father was the shepherd of the Chosen People, which signified the importance of the shepherd, his accountability for his flock, and the punishment for failing to care for the flock. We see this in passages such as Jeremiah 23:1-4, Jeremiah 25:32-38, and Ezekiel 34:1-6, and 10-16. No introductory material precedes this passage; in fact, it begins with the double amen, or "truly, truly," not otherwise seen at the beginning of His teachings in the Fourth Gospel. The structure strongly implies this passage continues from the previous chapter, John 9:39-41, which is the account of Jesus healing the man born blind.

The passage in chapter ten began when Jesus said, "Truly, truly I say to you," which meant that what followed was important. He then told a story about sheep to which many in the audience could immediately relate. The "you" in verse one referred to the Pharisees to whom He had been talking following the healing of the man born blind. Besides the vocational connections, the metaphor of sheep was frequent in the Old Testament, and sheep were also a frequent topic in rabbinical teachings.

The illustrative identity of sheep was always the nation of Israel or the Chosen People, and that was how Jesus used sheep in this instance. "This passage provides the closest parallel in the Fourth Gospel to the form and contents of any synoptic narrative parable." [121] In the word picture spoken by Jesus, several flocks of sheep had been gathered together for safety. Matthew, Mark, and Luke also contain many references to sheep and shepherds, which indicates the popularity of these settings. Even today, in the Middle East, shepherds still watch over sheep as they did at the time of Jesus.

At the time of Jesus, the role of the shepherd was considerably different than it is today. Instead of driving or using dogs to direct the sheep, the shepherd had individual names and calls for each of his sheep. He led the flock from place to place, and the sheep followed. The sheep knew his voice and only followed him. The sheep recognizing the voice of the shepherd was another safeguard against thieves or robbers. Even if someone else gained access to the sheep or overpowered the guard, because the sheep did not know the voice of the stranger, they would refuse to follow him. We can see the fondness the shepherd had for his sheep in His illustration of the lost sheep.

Because of the relationship between the shepherd and sheep, several shepherds could join their flocks together at night for protection. In this way, the shepherds could sleep and be confident their sheep were safe; several flocks slept together in a sheepfold with a gate across the entrance or with a hired hand to guard against predators. In this arrangement, the only way a predator could gain access to the sheep was over the wall. The next morning, each shepherd would call his sheep and lead them to pasture. "Curiously, the Greek text says that he not only 'leads them out' but also 'casts them out,' which might well be an ironic play on words of the fate of the man born blind, who was just cast out of the synagogue." [122]

This word picture of the shepherd leading his sheep may have been a hint or remez to Moses praying for a successor to lead the Israelites after his death. The person whom God chose to take the leadership role was Joshua. His name in Greek is Jesus. In verse seven, Jesus stressed the importance of His words with the double amen, or "truly, truly," to get their attention. Jesus presented Himself as the true shepherd of Judaism. Jesus "answered to all that was written of the Messiah, and took the path of God's will in presenting Himself to the people. He had been born of a virgin, of the covenant people, of the Judaic stock, in the royal city—Bethlehem. He had conformed to everything God required of an Israelite. He had been born under the Law. He was circumcised on the eighth day and subsequently, at the purification of His mother, He was presented to God in the Temple." [123]

At this point, the crowd faltered in their understanding of what Jesus was saying. The simple reason was they were not the sheep of His flock and were, therefore, unable to understand. By the time they comprehended what He was saying, their limited comprehension only served to harden their hearts against Him. Referring to the illustration of the sheep within the sheepfold, Jesus explained to the crowd that all who had come before Him were thieves and robbers. "The terms 'thief' and 'robber' overlap in meaning and may reflect Semitic parallelism, whereas 'thief' may focus on the covert nature of entrance and 'robber' on violence." [124] The thief and robber came to steal, kill, and destroy.

The triad of "steal," "kill," and "destroy" was a typical method of emphasis, whether good or bad. Another familiar triad in the New Testament is "faith," "love," and "hope." Within the confines of the sheepfold with the gate guarded, anyone other than the shepherd who sought access to the sheep by any means other than the gate would have been considered a thief and robber. "This account describes nothing less than the shepherd's right of ownership over the sheep; and consequently, at the same time, it describes his relationship to them, which is based on the right of ownership. For him, the way to them is not closed." [125]

This statement was dramatic but surely did not apply to all of the prophets of God scattered throughout the Old Testament. Rather, Jesus was "contrasting all false teaching in general to the Gospel and all false prophets to faithful teachers." [126] Boice echoes this comment and notes that "if He had, He would have been disparaging Moses, David, Solomon, and the long line of prophets. Jesus was not even referring to every teacher of religion outside of Judaism, for not all were thieves in the sense He intended. A thief is one who steals that which does not belong to him. And, since Jesus was talking about the way to God, a thief in this sense is one who steals Christ's honor by himself claiming to be the way." [127] As Dodd notes, the same class of criminal was in this discussion, and the fact that this teaching flowed directly from the sixth miracle, in which Jesus healed the man born blind, and His stern words for the Pharisees at the end of chapter nine support this premise. "The Pharisees have expelled from God's flock the man whom Christ Himself enlightened. They are scattering the sheep that Christ came to gather." [128]

Jesus could have also been addressing the Sadducees and the Scribes. The Sadducees found ways to make money through Temple activities and the sacrificial system while Scribes were condemned for covetousness. There were other religious leaders advocating armed insurrection, which almost always resulted in the death of the leader and many followers. All of these groups and leaders sought to claim the way. Thus, they were the thieves the true sheep would not recognize and from whom they would run away. Those who were truly His sheep would hear only His voice and follow only Him. Jesus repeated that He was the gate, and anyone who entered through Him would find pasture, which we should understand as meaning salvation.

Jesus then returned to the paradigm of the Good Shepherd, in contrast to the hireling. While it may be confusing to the modern reader and violate literary rules of character development, Jesus' audience would have understood the switching of roles in the illustration. The telling of stories and word pictures was the typical method of teaching for young and old alike, so Jesus' illustration about sheep, hirelings, and shepherds, confusing as it might be today, made perfect sense to the first-century audience. "The power of symbols lies, in part, in their flexibility and possibility to refocus attention. In this text, the meaning that is being emphasized is that Jesus represents authentic security for His people." [129]

The Good Shepherd would lay down his life for the sheep, as opposed to the hireling, who would run away. Jesus had shown He was the Good Shepherd through signs, teachings, and messianic prophecy. The principle Old Testament reference for this concept is most likely from Isaiah 53:4-7, which describes the suffering servant who was sacrificed for the sinful sheep. In contrast, the religious leaders had revealed their cruel and evil ways by excommunicating the man born blind whom Jesus had just healed (9:1-41).

The hirelings apparently wanted nothing at all to do with this particular "sheep," so he went to the true shepherd and became one of His sheep. At this point, the components of the illustration changed briefly. Initially, Jesus set the scene and described how the sheep would follow only the voice of their shepherd. He then gave Himself the role as the gate and implied some shepherds had failed in their responsibilities to the flock. Jesus then changed His role from that of the gate to that of the good shepherd.

The hireling in verse twelve, while he performed an important function to protect the sheep, was not held responsible for certain situations that may have occurred. Judaic law contained guidelines for the legal requirements of a hired shepherd. If a single wolf attacked a flock, the hired hand was duty-bound to defend the flock from the attack; however, if two or more wolves attacked, the hired hand could run away with no legal penalty because this was unavoidable. The hired hand would not receive blame, and compensation for any loss of sheep would not be mandated.

Following the premise that this illustration was a continuation of the healing of the man born blind, the hireling represented the Pharisees or Sadducees. "They were not true shepherds, but hirelings. They were only timeservers whose sole interest in the sheep was what they could get from the animals for themselves." [130] The welfare of the sheep was not a concern for the hireling because they were not his possessions. Jesus contrasted Himself as the opposite of the hireling who ran away, as the Good Shepherd who knew His sheep and whom the sheep knew, a different relationship than with the hireling. In verse fifteen, Jesus introduced a new thought that He would lay down His life for the sheep. This dramatic statement would have elicited a reaction of surprise or shock from the crowd because, at the time, it was exceedingly rare for a shepherd to die while guarding a flock. It was almost always an accident when a shepherd died in the line of duty because sheep were not considered sufficiently valuable for a man to die. The hireling wanted to live to collect his wages, not be killed and mourned.

The references to the gate and Good Shepherd in verse fourteen both also referred to salvation. In the same way as the gate, Jesus was the only path to salvation. As a shepherd, Jesus cared for the sheep of His flock and provided for their safety—to the extent that He would lay down His life for His sheep. Being the only gate, those who came in another way other than the gate were thieves and robbers. This passage is a parenthetical inclusion by the Apostle John to explain the events that were occurring. The verse notes the people to whom Jesus spoke did not understand. Brown notes in Matthew, Mark, and Luke the objections from His detractors had as the target the kingdom of heaven, but, in the Fourth Gospel, the detractors targeted Jesus. As the single subject of John's Gospel, this should not be surprising. In response to the objections of the crowd, Jesus explained the illustration.

Jesus introduced a new idea to His listeners in verse sixteen. Almost out of nowhere, He told them of other sheep "not of this sheep pen." Most scholars agree this was a reference to people who were not Jewish. We should see this passage as a precursor to the mystery revealed to the Apostle Paul, that Gentiles would be allowed to know Jesus as Lord and Savior. "The earliest distinction is offered by the Jewish Christian community, whose shepherd Jesus was from the beginning, and the Gentile believers, from the perspective of His earthly life; He will turn them into a single flock only in the future so that the distinction between them will disappear." [131]

The result of Jesus gathering other sheep, not of this fold was that all the sheep would become one flock with one shepherd. Jesus repeated a recurring theme here affirming that He would lay His life down for His sheep. He also spoke of this in verses eleven and fifteen. The death of Jesus was the will of God, and, because He was devoted to the will of the Father, Jesus would proceed to His death. The death of Jesus is linked here and other places with the resurrection, but to have resurrection a death must occur. Because of the resurrection, death is not the end but victory.

In verse eighteen, the Apostle John clearly describes Jesus as in complete control of every situation, even one that involves His death. Therefore, His death on the cross was not the result of actions by His enemies, the Roman Empire, or the religious leaders. No power on heaven or earth could have taken His life. Instead, He voluntarily gave up His life on the cross. Three days later, He took it up again, rose from the grave, and spent forty days with the disciples before His ascension.

Despite these criticisms of this apostle, we can note three things in Peter's defense. First, none of the other disciples, except Peter, followed Jesus after His arrest; second, he loved Jesus as his actions plainly revealed; and third, he tried to defend Jesus. Despite these virtues, it is somewhat amazing Peter chose to remain associated with the other disciples after his actions in the courtyard. Yet he was one of the first to run to the tomb of Jesus when it was reported the Lord's body was missing. It is doubtful whether Peter remembered that Jesus had foretold of his three denials and that he could not follow Him now, but he would follow Him later. This short passage of the words of Jesus is yet another indication of His divinity because He knew Peter would fail Him three times, yet would follow later.

After the resurrection and several post-resurrection appearances to the disciples and others, Jesus spent some of His last moments with the disciples. In his conversation with Peter, Jesus revealed His love for Peter, restored him to his position, and gave him new responsibilities as recorded in John 21:15-19. This passage reveals how Simon Peter, after leaving the ministry like the other disciples, was drawn back to service and his role as a disciple by a loving Savior who gave Peter his marching orders in the form of the three parts – feeding sheep, feeding lambs, and guiding the sheep.

CHAPTER FIFTEEN

THE SEVENTH SIGN
THE RESURRECTION OF LAZARUS

JOHN 11:1-44

The seventh sign of Jesus happened only a few short weeks before Jesus went to Jerusalem for what would be His last Passover. This sign, which confounded the religious leaders, was the greatest demonstration of Jesus' authority; even death could not thwart Him. Because of the significance of the sign, the Apostle John devotes virtually an entire chapter to the event, describing in rich detail the actions, thoughts, and implications of Jesus restoring Lazarus from the grave.

The resurrection of Lazarus brought the religious leaders to the point of no return because His claims put Him on a par with God. Passages like Genesis 30:22, Deuteronomy

28:12, and Ezekiel 27:13 stipulated that God "held the three great keys: the key to open the heavens and give rain; the key to open the womb and give conception; and the key to open the grave and raise the dead." [132] The narrative begins by identifying the players: Lazarus, the man who was sick, Martha, the older sister, and Mary, the younger.

The name "Lazarus" is a shortened version of "Eleazar," which comes from the Hebrew name El'azar meaning "whom God helps." Some critics point out similarities between this passage and the parable Jesus spoke of the Rich Man and Lazarus (Luke 16:19-31). For example, Luke 16:30, "corresponds precisely to John 11:45-53, where the Jews, who are unprepared to repent, resolve to kill Lazarus, who was raised from the dead, and Jesus who raised him from the dead." [133]

Despite this criticism, there is insufficient evidence to question the validity of this sign. At the time of Jesus, Eleazar was a common name. Martha was an Aramaic name meaning "lady," while Mary was the Greek form of the Hebrew Miriam. Three individuals each having a name from a different culture was not unusual at the time of Jesus and was indicative of the intermingling of the cultures. Mary was the same woman who later anointed the head of Jesus with spikenard ointment and wiped His feet with her hair (John 12:3). Matthew 26:6-13 and Mark 14:3-9 also mention Mary's act of pouring costly perfume on Jesus. The two sisters appear in Luke 10:38-42, which provides additional insight into the two women. Pink makes an observation that each time the New Testament mentions Mary; she was at the feet of Jesus, listening to His words or worshipping.

Lazarus is unknown to the reader, so the passage provides his identification based on his sisters. According to the narrative, he became ill, and his condition became increasingly severe, to the point his sisters sought assistance. "It is lovely to note that the sisters' message included no request to Jesus to come to Bethany. They knew that was unnecessary; they knew that the simple statement that they were in need would bring Him to them." [134] The wording of the sisters' message indicated a state of weakness and failing health to the point of death. The same wording can be found describing the man infirm for thirty-eight years at the pool in Jerusalem. Whitacre notes the message sent to Jesus is similar to the request of Mary when the wedding party in Cana had exhausted the supply of wine. Neither the two sisters nor the mother of Jesus told Jesus how to respond but presented the problem for Him to resolve.

The sisters probably assumed Jesus would immediately come to Bethany to help Lazarus. "Human love would have hurried with all speed to Bethany, if possible, to arrive before death set in. Divine love acts otherwise, and also have the divine knowledge for its work." [135] As typical for Jesus, He confounded everyone by delaying His departure. Calvin observes that when the works of God more closely resembled normal events in nature, people were more likely to reject them and diminish the glory to God. It is critical to the interpretation of this sign to understand the timeline. There is no indication in the passage that Jesus was under any compulsion, yet He remained where He was two days. "The delay of Jesus to replying to the urgent plea of the sisters is difficult to explain on any ground other than that of His complete mastery of death." [136]

Jesus' response is also puzzling since He did not mean the sickness was not fatal, but rather a sickness would not end in death. Jesus' response was like His reaction to His mother when she came to Him at the wedding in Cana, and He refused to provide assistance. Jesus could have healed Lazarus from where He was, as He had done for the son of the royal official, but He chose to travel to Bethany to heal, recognizing the event as an opportunity to glorify His Father. Jesus knew what would happen, and His actions would glorify God, which would glorify the Son.

Brown comments the statements and actions of Jesus in this sign contain several plays on words. The sickness would not end in death because Jesus would give physical life, which represents eternal life. The life Jesus restored to Lazarus would glorify Him but would also lead to His death, which was the catalyst for eternal life for those who believe in His name. Knowing the words of Jesus could be misinterpreted as being uncaring or willing to allow Lazarus to die for His purposes; John mentions several times the love of Jesus toward Lazarus, Martha, and Mary. This phrasing is necessary is because we—

today just as at the time of Jesus— "generally interpret any delay in rendering help as cruel because of our perspectives on the avoidance of all pain and because of our general commitment to the immediacy of action as it pertains to time." [137]

While some commentaries suggest Jesus and His disciples were near the Jordan River due east of Jerusalem when they received the message, the timeline of the narrative and the distances involved strongly suggest the location was Batanea, approximately ninety miles north-east of Jerusalem. The logic behind this premise is that when the messenger delivered Jesus the news about Lazarus, Jesus commented the sickness would not end in death but was intended for the glory of God. This statement implies Lazarus was still alive at the time. Two days later, Jesus said Lazarus had fallen asleep, which was another illustration of His divine knowledge. If Jesus and His disciples were in Batanea, the timeline supports the premise of Lazarus having not yet died when Jesus received the message.

Given the hilly and rough terrain of Judea, the distance a person could walk would have been about thirty miles. Taking all these factors into account, the passage suggests Lazarus was alive when Jesus received the message. He and the disciples remained at Batanea for two days and then set out for Bethany. Since it took the group three days to travel the ninety miles to Bethany, it is easy to construct a timeline that does not contradict the words of Jesus.

In this scenario, Lazarus died the day after the message of his illness reached Jesus. Lazarus died on the first day that Jesus and the disciples were in Batanea. Martha and Mary, along with the other inhabitants of Bethany and anyone who came from Jerusalem, held the funeral and followed with a period of mourning. Burial on the day of death was common because there were no means of preserving the corpse. In keeping with the usual activities of the day, they wrapped Lazarus in grave clothes and spices and placed his body in a crypt, or cave. A stone was placed at the opening and mourning—partially provided by professional mourners—continued for a time.

Jesus waited one more day and then led the disciples on the three-day trek to Bethany. This timeline, logical and complete, explains how Lazarus could have been alive when Jesus received the message, the delay in His going to Bethany, and the four days Lazarus was in the tomb before Jesus arrived on the scene. This timeline does not account for the time the messenger took to deliver the message to Jesus. Granted, it is hard to understand the actions of Jesus at this point in the narrative, but "it is much more probable that John wants us to see Jesus as moved by no external forces, but solely by His determination to do the will of God." [138]

Jesus kept His intentions from the disciples until it was time to depart for Bethany. When He announced His plans to travel to Judea, the response of the disciples was immediate and negative because of the confrontation at the Feast of Dedication between Jesus and the religious leaders. Because of the dangerous situation in Judea, the group was in Batanea, which was out of the jurisdictional authority of the religious leaders. Ridderbos explains that if this sign occurred in March of CE 33 and the Feast of Dedication (Chapter 10) occurred in the previous December, the disciples' comments that the Jews had been "just now" seeking to stone Jesus (verse 8) was an exaggeration. Now, to their dismay, Jesus was announcing plans to return.

Despite their objections, Jesus was adamant to travel to Bethany, located east of the Mount of Olives, about two miles from the capital city. In response to the disciples, Jesus noted there are twelve hours in the day, and if anyone walks in the day, he does not stumble because of the light of the world. These words were meant for the disciples, for as long as Jesus, the light of the world, was with them, they could see where they were going and protected from stumbling that could occur when walking without the light.

He continued this thought by contrasting walking in the light with stumbling because the one who walks in the night stumbles because the light is not in him. This allusion to action during the light is quite similar to His comments before healing the man born blind in chapter nine. As in many other instances in the Fourth Gospel, John is making a double reference to natural light and the spiritual light which is Jesus. Again, John presents Jesus as the light of the world, and when His light is taken away, men stumble in the darkness.

Jesus then focused His attention on the purpose of going to Bethany, which was because Lazarus had fallen asleep—a euphemism for death—and He was going to awaken him. Notice in verse eleven how Jesus referred to Lazarus as "our" friend, referring to Himself and the disciples but switched to the singular "I" when speaking of awakening Lazarus. In their typical response, the disciples—as they did so frequently with Jesus—took Him literally and commented that it was a good thing Lazarus was asleep since it would enable him to more quickly recover. The disciples evidently believed there was "no need for going to Lazarus, since sleep is, according to Jewish notions, one of the six, or according to others, five symptoms or crises in recovery from dangerous illness." [139]

Jesus explained to the disciples that Lazarus had died and, in fact, was glad He had not been there so His followers would more deeply believe. "The Lord was not glad because Lazarus was dead. That would have been heartless given the sorrow of his sisters. He was glad because He knew the outcome. He was going to 'awaken him.'" [140] Some scholars question the metaphor of sleep, suggesting it was not common at the time of Jesus. However, several verses, Deuteronomy 31:16, 1

Kings 2:10, and Daniel 12:2 for example, include the metaphor of sleep as death, so the expression was not foreign to the disciples.

The same mention of sleep is used to indicate the death of Stephen, the first martyr. John is careful in verse fourteen to separate the symbolic or allegorical words of Jesus of the previous verses with the blunt statement of Lazarus being dead. The aorist tense of His statement indicates death had taken place. With these blunt words, the group departed for Bethany. The disciples, as evident by the comments by Thomas, thought to return with Jesus to Judea and die with Him.

"Thomas ironically understands Jesus correctly; for Jesus to raise Lazarus will cost Him His life, and Thomas and the other disciples should (though will not) follow Him to the cross." [141] Some find it surprising Thomas emerged here as a leader and expressed the unspoken consensus of the group, but given his seemingly melancholy nature, this should not be surprising. The same Thomas said that unless he could touch the nail holes and place his hand into the side of Jesus (John 20:25), he would not believe. They expected they would die when the religious leaders found Jesus was once again within their jurisdiction. However, they were devoted to Jesus and were willing to die with Him.

The scene shifts in verse seventeen with the arrival of Jesus at Bethany. The passage reveals a couple of important facts: first, Lazarus had been dead for four days; and second, Bethany was only a couple of miles from Jerusalem, and many who lived in the capital city knew of the death and had come to console Martha and Mary. "That many Jews should be present at Lazarus' 'wake' is exactly in keeping with ancient custom in which almost an entire village could turn out to mourn the death of one of its families' members." [142] Because of this custom, "everyone who could was supposed, in courtesy and respect, to join the procession on its way.

One curious custom was that the women walked first, for it was held that since woman by her first sin brought death into the world, she ought to lead the mourners to the tomb." [143] The fact that many came from Jerusalem indicates the prominence of the family in Jewish society. As John reveals in the next chapter, Mary pouring expensive perfume on Jesus while He was at supper suggests the family was wealthy, which contributed to their prominence.

The fact Lazarus had been dead four days is of critical importance to the Jews. "The spirit of the departed was thought to hover around the body for three days in the hope of resuscitation. The raising of Lazarus after four days, then, would be clearly seen as a manifestation of the glory of God, which would strengthen the two sisters' faith." [144] Jewish writing from the early third century CE states "the mourners should continue to come to the tomb for three days because the dead person continues to be present. Mourning is at its height on the third day, presumably because it is the last time the dead person will be present there." [145] On the fourth day, the spirit departed forever, and death was accepted as permanent because of the decomposition of the corpse. The spirit went to Sheol, the place of the dead, where it awaited resurrection.

Martha, upon hearing Jesus was in the vicinity, went to welcome Him. This reaction on her part should not be surprising as the Scriptures reveal her as assertive, likely a type A personality, while her sister, Mary, was quiet and more reserved. Regardless of her personality, Keener notes the fact that Martha went to Jesus revealed great respect for Him as her actions were the opposite of normal social behavior for the bereaved and consoler. The opening words of Martha reflected her character; if He had been there, her brother would not have died. Her words have been seen as both a statement of faith in the ability of Jesus to heal as well as regret that He was not able to arrive sooner to save her brother. Her words are not construed to contain rebuke, only regret of His late arrival.

While she had faith in Jesus to restore health to the sick, Jesus' power or authority to raise the dead was beyond her. The conversation with Jesus would confirm her contention that the grave, especially after four days, was an insurmountable barrier. She continued her profession of faith (verse twenty-two) that whatever He asked of God, God would grant Him. Scholars are divided on the meaning of this verse, but it is likely a mixture of continued expression of faith in Jesus with a normal limit, nonetheless a faith she was willing to expand. We must remember as we examine these verses that we know the rest of the story. For Martha, this was uncharted territory in her walk of faith; we should commend her faith; her confusion is understandable and forgivable.

The words of Jesus "about not dying is emphatic, using a double negative. This remark turns the coming miracle into a teaching about Jesus' authority to give unending life." [146] The statement Jesus spoke that her brother would rise again was misunderstood by Martha to mean the resurrection at the end of time. A vast majority of Jews at the time of Jesus did believe in a future physical resurrection. Martha apparently held this belief as well, but she was also unaware of what Jesus meant when He said He was the resurrection. Borchert notes the words of Jesus about her brother's coming resurrection contain another instance of the double meanings often found in the Fourth Gospel, which include two births, two temples, and two waters. In these verses, John uses His conversation with Martha about two resurrections to reveal more about Jesus the Messiah.

Her positive response, even though she misunderstood His intent, indicates she was a Pharisee because this was one of the beliefs of this Jewish sect (as opposed to the Sadducees who did not believe in the resurrection). As Dodd notes, "it seems that Martha is here playing the usual part assigned to interlocutors in Johannine dialogues; she is misunderstanding a saying of Jesus to open the way to further explication." [147] Martha's statement, while expressing faith in Jesus and resurrection on the last day, revealed she was not contemplating an imminent resurrection of Lazarus. In other words, the two were conversing, but on different levels of meaning. While we can find a couple of instances of someone being brought back to life in the Old Testament, nowhere had it been recorded of a person four days dead returning to life.

After speaking to Jesus, Martha departed to tell Mary of Jesus' proximity. When Mary heard the news, she departed immediately to meet with Jesus, not telling the others her destination. The mourners assumed she was going to Lazarus, but, going ahead of the mourners; she went to Jesus. The meeting between the two was briefer than that between her sister and Jesus. Mary fell at His feet and was more emotional than her sister. Her words were more pointed and less tactful than her sister. Like Martha, she believed Lazarus would not have died had Jesus been there; her words seem to contain more reproach than those of Martha, but this may have been a reflection of her more agitated state of mind. Her faith and understanding of the power of Jesus were identical to Martha's. Yes, Jesus could heal the sick and infirm, but the curtains of death were beyond Him.

Jesus, seeing Mary and the Jews weeping, was troubled. He asked Mary where they had buried Lazarus. As was typical at the time, the deceased were buried a distance away so the living would not become ceremonially unclean. Upon His request, she took Him to the cave where there were commotion and intense expressions of grief and sorrow. The scene deeply moved Jesus. The verse indicates Jesus made a loud, indistinguishable noise, somewhat like a horse snorting. When ascribed to a person, it infers anger, which is how many commentaries understand it, begging the question as to the focus of His wrath.

It could not have been the untimely death of Lazarus because He previously explained the purpose to His disciples and knew any mourning would be short-lived. Some interpret His anger as being toward death and all it implies but is likely more conjecture than solid exegesis. Another suggestion is the flute players and wailing women lamenting the death of Lazarus as the end of his existence angered Him. While some of these explanations may be feasible, the reality is we do not know the reason for the strong emotions shown by Jesus.

He then asked Martha and Mary the location of the grave, and the sisters escorted Him to the site. Upon arriving at the cave, John records the shortest verse in the Bible: "Jesus wept." John uses a word for the tears of Jesus not found anywhere else in the New Testament. In describing Jesus in such a way, he strives to ensure his readers do not mistake the meaning, which is different from the word for the crying of the other mourners at the cave. The word describes the weeping of Jesus as quiet and subdued but no less intense. Commentators have made suggestions about the reason He was so moved. Since He was about to raise Lazarus, the reason could not have been his death. Interestingly, Judas Iscariot has a similar emotion in the next chapter as John recounts his reaction to Mary pouring expensive perfume on the head of Jesus at the house of Simon the Leper.

As was typically the case, the onlookers misinterpreted the actions of Jesus. At the cave, two groups of people were present: those who saw His tears and marveled at the love Jesus expressed for Lazarus and others who wondered why He could not have saved Lazarus from death. Taking control of the situation, Jesus commanded the people to roll away the stone in front of the cave. Martha, ever the practical of the two sisters, questioned Jesus, noting the corpse would have a foul odor. Embalming was not the usual practice, and the corpse decomposing would have produced an unpleasant, pungent odor. This question further indicates her faith was not to the point that she understood Jesus meant an immediate resurrection of her brother.

The perfect tense of the words in this verse indicates the permanence of Lazarus' condition. There is no indication whether the cave was horizontal, with the stone lying on top of the opening, or vertical, with the stone resting against the opening, but both arrangements were common at the time of Jesus. If the grave were an opening in the side of a hill or mountain, as Barclay explains, it would have been a room about six feet by nine feet by ten feet tall with three shelves cut into the two sides of the cave and two shelves cut out of the wall facing the door. It was also typical for there to be one or two steps down into the cave so a person would descend entering the tomb. A large stone in the shape of a wheel would be in a groove along the front of the cave so to roll aside to allow other bodies into the cave. Overruling her objection, Jesus reminded Martha of His earlier words. These words Jesus spoke here are not recorded in the Fourth Gospel but are likely similar to those He spoke to Martha when they conversed earlier. Martha, having the authority of the closest living relative, consented to the command of Jesus, and they remove the stone.

Once the stone was out of the way, Jesus looked up to heaven and referred to God as "Father," not using the word "our" to include the Jews around Him, but as His Father, indicating the exclusive relationship He had with God. His words were first of thanksgiving but then referred to an earlier prayer; this prayer initiated the restoration of life to Lazarus. Jesus offered thanksgiving so those hearing His voice would understand His relationship with the Father and that God had sent him.

Again, John depicted Jesus as dependent upon the Father and focused on giving glory to God. The prayer of Jesus, spoken for the benefit of others, was to glorify the Father. At the conclusion of His prayer, Jesus called out with a loud voice, "Lazarus, come forth." As with the prayer, the exclamation was so the people present would not think Jesus was performing magic or casting some incantation but calling Lazarus by name and giving a specific command. This sign was the magnificent fulfillment of His prophecy, as recounted in John 5:25-30, that those who heard His words and believed would live.

Behold, the man Lazarus, still wrapped in burial clothing emerged from the cave. As a note of explanation, people laid the deceased on a burial sheet wide enough to be wrapped and twice as long as the length of the body. The sheet wrapped from the feet, over the head, and back down to the feet. The mourners would add spices to the wrapping, and use cords or strips of burial cloth to bind the feet and the arms to the torso. They would also wrap a separate burial cloth around the head. This wrapping was still on Lazarus when he came forth from the cave because Jesus commanded the burial wrapping be removed and to release Lazarus. "The physical life that returns to a rotting body is only a feeble reflection of that true life which Jesus calls forth in believers.

A Puritan writer made the wry observation that had Jesus not said 'Lazarus' referring to a unique individual, everyone buried within earshot of His voice would have risen from the dead at the command of the Son of God. Since there was only one 'Lazarus' within hearing distance of Jesus, he was the only one raised. The powerful cry with which Jesus calls Lazarus out of the grace is only an external echo of the call with which He, God's messenger, calls all men who believe in Him to God's life." [148] As a result of this sign, John notes many who had come to comfort Martha and Mary believed in Jesus, which was the entire purpose of His raising Lazarus from the dead; others, however, reported the event to the Pharisees and religious leaders.

That Jesus raised Lazarus from the dead dramatically refuted the arguments of the Pharisees and religious leaders. There could be virtually no doubt that Jesus was whom He claimed, and the religious leaders were even more afraid of His message and the damage to their religious world. For these reasons, the intensity on the part of the religious leaders to remove Jesus from the scene became more acute. The religious leaders also considered doing away with Lazarus because of what Jesus had done. The religious leaders accomplished their goals a short time after this sign with the false trial and crucifixion of Jesus.

Bibliography

[1] Kysar, Robert, *John, The Maverick Gospel*, Page 97.

[2] Witherington, III, Ben, *John's Wisdom*, Page 94.

[3] Kostenberger, Andreas, *Baker Evangelical Commentary of the New Testament – John,* Page 120.

[4] Bultmann, Rudolf, *The Gospel of John, A Commentary*, Page 135.

[5] Edersheim, Alfred, *The Life and Times of Jesus the Messiah,* Page 265.

[6] Schnackenburg, Rudolf, *The Gospel According to St. John, Volume One*, Page 373.

[7] Neyrey, Jerome, *The Gospel of John*, Page 79.

[8] Barclay, William, *Daily Bible Study Series – John, Volume One*, Page 129.

[9] Neyrey, Jerome, *The Gospel of John*, Page 63.

[10] Bultmann, Rudolf, *The Gospel of John, A Commentary*, Pages 118-19.

[11] Kruse, Colin, *Tyndale New Testament Commentaries – John*, Page 91.

[12] Carson, D. A., *Pillar New Testament Commentary – John,* Page 169.

[13] Blomberg, Craig, *Jesus and the Gospel*, Page 225.

[14] Schnackenburg, Rudolf, *The Gospel According to St. John, Volume One*, Page 328.

[15] Haenchen, Ernst, *A Commentary on the Gospel of John, Volume One*, Page 173.

[16] Phillips, John, *Exploring the Gospel of John*, Page 53.

[17] Pink, Arthur, *Exposition of the Gospel of John*, Page 84.

---

[18] Bock, Darrell, *Jesus According to Scripture*, Page 425.

[19] Carson, D. A., *Pillar New Testament Commentary – John*, Page 168.

[20] Dodd, C.H., *The Interpretation of the Fourth Gospel*, Pag.e 299.

[21] Ridderbos, Herman, *The Gospel of John*, Page 107

[22] Hobbs, Herschel, *Bible Study Commentary – John*, Page 19.

[23] Ashton, John, *Understanding the Fourth Gospel*, Page 177.

[24] Blomberg, Craig, *Historical Reliability of John's Gospel*, Pages 85-6.

[25] Kruse, Colin, *Tyndale New Testament Commentaries – John*, Page 127.

[26] Borchert, Gerald L., *The New American Commentary – John, Volume One*, Page 201.

[27] Hobbs, Herschel, *Bible Study Commentary – John*, Page 23.

[28] Carson, D. A., *Pillar New Testament Commentary – John*, Page 217.

[29] Keener, Craig, *The Gospel of John, Volume One*, Page 593.

[30] Barclay, William, *Daily Bible Study Series – John, Volume One*, Page 151.

[31] Haenchen, Ernst, *A Commentary on the Gospel of John, Volume One*, Page 220.

[32] Morris, Leon, *New International Commentary on the New Testament – John,* Page 230.

[33] Ridderbos, Herman, *The Gospel of John*, Page 155.

[34] Hendriksen, William, *New Testament Commentary – John*, Page 164.

---

[35] Schnackenburg, Rudolf, *The Gospel According to St. John, Volume One*, Page 436.

[36] Keener, Craig, *The Gospel of John, Volume One*, Page 585.

[37] Carson, D. A., *Pillar New Testament Commentary – John*, Page 227.

[38] Keener, Craig, *The Gospel of John, Volume One*, Page 628.

[39] Hendriksen, William, *New Testament Commentary – John*, Page 181.

[40] Bruce, F.F., *The Gospel and Epistles of John*, Page 117.

[41] Barclay, William, *Daily Bible Study Series – John, Volume One*, Page 174.

[42] Calvin, John, *The Crossway Classic Commentary – John*, Page 113.

[43] Morris, Leon, *New International Commentary on the New Testament – John,* Page 256.

[44] Kruse, Colin, *Tyndale New Testament Commentaries – John*, Page 144.

[45] Borchert, Gerald L., *The New American Commentary – John, Volume One*, Page 217.

[46] Phillips, John, *Exploring the Gospel of John*, Page 97.

[47] Tenney, Merrill, *John, The Gospel of Belief*, Page 106.

[48] Whitacre, Rodney, *IVP New Testament Commentary Series – John*, Page 126.

[49] Ridderbos, Herman, *The Gospel of John*, Page 191.

[50] Lenski, R. C. H., *The Interpretation of St. John's Gospel,* Page 366.

[51] Brown, Raymond, *The Anchor Bible – John, Volume One*, Page 218.

---

[52] Bultmann, Rudolf, *The Gospel of John, A Commentary*, Page 256.

[53] Neyrey, Jerome, *The Gospel of John*, Page 108.

[54] Boice, James, *Foundations of the Christian Faith*, Page 306.

[55] Blomberg, Craig, *The Historical Reliability of John's Gospel*, Page 108.

[56] Neyrey, Jerome, *The Gospel of John*, Page 102.

[57] Whitacre, Rodney, *IVP New Testament Commentary Series – John*, Page 119.

[58] Kostenberger, Andreas, *Baker Evangelical Commentary of the New Testament – John,* Page 178.

[59] Dodd, C.H., *The Interpretation of the Fourth Gospel*, Page 329.

[60] Barclay, William, *Daily Bible Study Series – John, Volume One*, Page 179.

[61] Wiersbe, Warren, *NT Commentary – John, Volume One*, Page 78-79.

[62] Haenchen, Ernst, *A Commentary on the Gospel of John, Volume One*, Page 255.

[63] Lenski, R.C.H., *The Interpretation of St. John's Gospel*, Page 353.

[64] Barclay, William, *Daily Bible Study Series – John, Volume One*, Page 182.

[65] Boice, James, *Foundations of the Christian Faith*, Page 302.

[66] Borchert, Gerald L., *The New American Commentary – John, Volume One*, Page 229.

[67] Brown, Raymond, *The Anchor Bible – John, Volume One*, Page 217.

[68] Tenney, Merrill, *John, The Gospel of Belief*, Page 106.

[69] Kostenberger, Andreas, *Baker Evangelical Commentary of the New Testament – John,* Page 208.

[70] Brown, Raymond, *The Anchor Bible – John, Volume One*, Page 265.

[71] Anderson, Paul, *The Riddles of the Fourth Gospel*, Page 31.

[72] Dodd, C. H., *The Interpretation of the Fourth Gospel*, Page 335.

[73] Phillips, John, *Exploring the Gospel of John*, Page 127.

[74] Bock, Darrell, *Jesus According to Scripture*, Page 450.

[75] Haenchen, Ernst, *A Commentary on the Gospel of John, Volume One*, Page 291.

[76] Whitacre, Rodney, *IVP New Testament Commentary Series – John*, Page 158.

[77] Kruse, Colin, *Tyndale New Testament Commentaries – John*, Page 172.

[78] Lenski, R. C. H., *The Interpretation of St. John's Gospel,* Page 462.

[79] Morris, Leon, *New International Commentary on the New Testament – John,* Page 335.

[80] Dodd, C. H., *The Interpretation of the Fourth Gospel*, Page 328.

[81] Ridderbos, Herman, *The Gospel of John*, Page 213.

[82] Bock, Darrell, *Jesus According to Scripture*, Page 437.

[83] Blomberg, Craig, *The Historical Reliability of John's Gospel*, Page 120.

[84] Whitacre, Rodney, *IVP New Testament Commentary Series – John*, Page 142.

[85] Kruse, Colin, *Tyndale New Testament Commentaries – John*, Page 161.

---

[86] Hendriksen, William, *New Testament Commentary – John*, Page 216.

[87] Bruce, F.F., *The Gospel and Epistles of John*, Page 146.

[88] Calvin, John, *The Crossway Classic Commentary – John*, Page 149.

[89] Bock, Darrell, *Jesus According to Scripture*, Page 45.

[90] Ridderbos, Herman, *The Gospel of John*, Page 262.

[91] Pink, Arthur, *Exposition of the Gospel of John*, Page 392.

[92] Keener, Craig, *The Gospel of John, Volume One*, Page 714.

[93] Boice, James, *Foundations of the Christian Faith*, Page 353.

[94] Brown, Raymond, *The Anchor Bible – John, Volume One*, Page 253.

[95] Tenney, Merrill, *John, The Gospel of Belief*, Page 114.

[96] Morris, Leon, *New International Commentary on the New Testament – John,* Page 307.

[97] Ridderbos, Herman, *The Gospel of John*, Page 217.

[98] Hendriksen, William, *New Testament Commentary – John*, Page 226.

[99] Bruce, F. F., *The Gospel and Epistles of John*, Page 191.

[100] Lenski, R. C. H., *The Interpretation of St. John's Gospel,* Page 592.

[101] Morris, Leon, *New International Commentary on the New Testament – John,* Page 397.

[102] Ridderbos, Herman, *The Gospel of John*, Page 302.

[103] Bruce, F. F., *The Gospel and Epistles of John*, Page 195.

[104] Tenney, Merrill, *John, The Gospel of Belief*, Page 146.

[105] Schnackenburg, Rudolf, *The Gospel According to St. John, Volume Two*, Page 206.

[106] Kruse, Colin, *Tyndale New Testament Commentaries – John*, Page 209.

[107] Brown, Raymond, *The Anchor Bible – John, Volume One*, Page 361.

[108] Barclay, William, *Daily Bible Study Series – John, Volume Two*, Page 23.

[109] Keener, Craig, *The Gospel of John, Volume One*, Page 777.

[110] Kostenberger, Andreas, *Baker Evangelical Commentary of the New Testament – John,* Page 283.

[111] Lenski, R.C.H., *The Interpretation of St. John's Gospel*, Page 661.

[112] Brown, Raymond, *The Anchor Bible – John, Volume One*, Page 381.

[113] Bultmann, Rudolf, *The Gospel of John, A Commentary*, Page 333.

[114] Schnackenburg, Rudolf, *The Gospel According to St. John, Volume Two*, Page 247.

[115] Edersheim, Alfred, *The Life and Times of Jesus the Messiah*, Page 600.

[116] Blomberg, Craig, *Jesus and the Gospels*, Page 298.

[117] Calvin, John, *The Crossway Classic Commentary – John*, Page 244.

[118] Bruce, F.F., *The Gospel and Epistles of John*, Page 219.

[119] Kostenberger, Andreas, *Baker Evangelical Commentary of the New Testament – John,* Page 278.

[120] Edersheim, Alfred, *The Life and Times of Jesus the Messiah,* Page 634.

[121] Blomberg, *Jesus and the Gospel*, Page 158.

[122] Neyrey, Jerome, *The Gospel of John*, Page 178.

[123] Pink, Arthur, *Exposition of the Gospel of John*, Pages 103-104.

[124] Kostenberger, Andreas, *Baker Evangelical Commentary of the New Testament – John,* Page 300.

[125] Bultmann, Rudolf, *The Gospel of John, A Commentary*, Page 372.

[126] Calvin, John, *The Crossway Classic Commentary – John*, Page 253.

[127] Boice, James, *Foundations of the Christian Faith,* Page 634.

[128] Dodd, C. H., *The Interpretation of the Fourth Gospel*, Page 35.

[129] Borchert, Gerald L., *The New American Commentary – John, Volume One*, Page 334.

[130] Hobbs, Herschel, *Bible Study Commentary – John*, Page 50.

[131] Haenchen, Ernst, *A Commentary on the Gospel of John, Volume Two*, Page 49.

[132] Wiersbe, Warren, *NT Commentary – John, Volume One*, Page 83.

[133] Haenchen, Ernst, *A Commentary on the Gospel of John, Volume Two*, Page 69.

[134] Barclay, William, *Daily Bible Study Series – John, Volume Two*, Page 81.

[135] Lenski, R.C.H., *The Interpretation of St. John's Gospel*, Page 762.

[136] Tenney, Merrill, *John, The Gospel of Belief*, Page 172.

[137] Borchert, Gerald L., *The New American Commentary – John, Volume One*, Page 351.

[138] Morris, Leon, *New International Commentary on the New Testament – John,* Page 480.

[139] Edersheim, Alfred, *The Life and Times of Jesus the Messiah*, Page 692.

[140] Phillips, John, *Exploring the Gospel of John*, Pages 211-2.

[141] Keener, Craig, *The Gospel of John, Volume Two,* Page 842.

[142] Blomberg, Craig, *The Historical Reliability of John's Gospel*, Page 167.

[143] Barclay, William, *Daily Bible Study Series – John, Volume Two*, Page 89.

[144] Kruse, Colin, *Tyndale New Testament Commentaries – John*, Page 248.

[145] Whitacre, Rodney, *IVP New Testament Commentary Series – John*, Page 283.

[146] Bock, Darrell, *Jesus According to Scripture*, Pages 479-80.

[147] Dodd, C.H., *The Interpretation of the Fourth Gospel,* Page 364.

[148] Schnackenburg, Rudolf, *The Gospel According to St. John, Volume Two*, Page 331.

38062003R00120

Printed in Poland
by Amazon Fulfillment
Poland Sp. z o.o., Wrocław